The
Cultural Proficiency
Journey

I heartwarmingly dedicate this book to my father, JW Jones, Sr. Although never receiving a formal education, he taught me the more important things in life—love, honor, and respect.

—Franklin

I dedicate this book to my courageous mom, Earnestine Bowie Wilson. Because of a moral choice she made at 16 years old, I am here today to make this contribution to our children and families who we serve for generations to come.

—Brenda

Kikanza J. Nuri-Robins for being who she is in my life.

—Randy

The Cultural Proficiency *Journey*

Moving Beyond Ethical Barriers Toward Profound School Change

Franklin CampbellJones
Brenda CampbellJones
Randall B. Lindsey

Foreword by Linda C. Tillman

CORWIN
A SAGE Company

For information:

Corwin
A SAGE Company
2455 Teller Road
Thousand Oaks, California 91320
(800) 233–9936
Fax: (800) 417–2466
www.corwin.com

SAGE Ltd.
1 Oliver's Yard
55 City Road
London EC1Y 1SP
United Kingdom

SAGE India Pvt. Ltd.
B 1/I 1 Mohan Cooperative
   Industrial Area
Mathura Road, New Delhi 110 044
India

SAGE Asia-Pacific Pte. Ltd.
33 Pekin Street #02-01
Far East Square
Singapore 048763

Printed in the United States of America.

Library of Congress Cataloging-in-Publication Data

CampbellJones, Franklin.
The cultural proficiency journey: moving beyond ethical barriers toward profound school change/Franklin CampbellJones, Brenda CampbellJones, Randall B. Lindsey.
     p. cm.
Includes bibliographical references and index.
ISBN 978-1-4129-7794-4 (pbk.)
    1. Multicultural education—United States. 2. School improvement programs—United States. 3. Educational leadership—United States. I. CampbellJones, Brenda. II. Lindsey, Randall B. III. Title.

LC1099.3.C365 2010
370.1170973—dc22   2009035963

This book is printed on acid-free paper.

          12   13   14   10   9   8   7   6   5   4   3

Acquisitions Editor:	Dan Alpert
Associate Editor:	Megan Bedell
Production Editor:	Eric Garner
Copy Editor:	Nancy Conger
Typesetter:	C&M Digitals (P) Ltd.
Proofreader:	Carole Quandt
Indexer:	Judy Hunt
Cover Designer:	Rose Storey

Contents

Foreword

Educators are called upon to teach every child, regardless of race, class, gender, disability, or other markers of difference. This imperative has become more important in the rapidly changing contexts of U.S. society and education. No longer a monolithic society dominated by a single race, the United States is now populated with individuals from numerous races and ethnicities. So too are schools in every context—urban, rural, and suburban. Thus, race and culture have increasingly become a central focus in the education of children in U.S. public schools.

The increased diversity in schools raises numerous questions about how teachers teach, students learn, and leaders lead. Among these questions are: What are the most effective instructional techniques needed to educate students from diverse backgrounds? What levels of cultural knowledge do teachers and leaders need to educate children from diverse backgrounds? What levels of cultural competency do teachers and leaders need to educate children from diverse backgrounds? In what ways can schools fulfill their responsibility to educate every child? These and other questions are addressed in this book. CampbellJones and colleagues clearly articulate the bottom line for meeting the social, emotional, and educational needs of all children: Schools as organizational structures and the educators in them must confront and change negative beliefs, attitudes, and behaviors toward students who have long been considered "other people's children."

As the authors correctly point out, cultural proficiency is a framework for guiding schools and school systems toward policies, practices, and procedures that lead to an excellent and equitable education for all children, rather than for selected students. In my own experiences as a teacher, administrator, and now as a university professor, I have seen teachers and leaders struggle with how to effectively educate all children, and particularly children from diverse backgrounds. This has especially been the case in districts with a significant number of schools where students of color represent the majority of the populations, and school districts with large influxes of immigrants. Thus, race and its companion dilemma, class, have in many districts fueled teachers' (and sometimes parents') resistance to viewing every child as worthy of the best possible education and their best efforts. These issues point to the need for cultural proficiency at all levels of education, but especially in the classroom.

This book is timely and much needed. The cultural proficiency framework represents a foundation for gaining knowledge and skills that will help teachers and leaders not only to become culturally proficient, but to view cultural proficiency as integral to good teaching and effective leadership. The practical examples, the exercises, and the opportunities for reflection all serve to guide the reader to a better understanding of the importance of cultural proficiency in instructional and leadership practices. Rather than a one-time professional development exercise or the next new buzz word, the book emphasizes that cultural proficiency must become part of the philosophy and mission of schools.

The essence of the book can be summed up in the authors' five essential elements of cultural competency—namely, that teachers and leaders are competent when they believe in and have a commitment to social justice, advocacy, the mentoring of underserved students for access to educational opportunity, the mentoring of more privileged students for historical awareness of inequity, and a commitment to leveling the educational and societal playing field for all students regardless of race, class, gender, disability, or other markers of difference. Armed with these commitments, teachers and leaders can fulfill their responsibility to educate every child.

—Linda C. Tillman, PhD
University of North Carolina, Chapel Hill

Preface

Our deepest fear is not that we are inadequate. Our deepest fear is that we are powerful beyond measure. It is our light, not our darkness that most frightens us.

—Marianne Williamson, p. 190

Establishing a moral compass is at the heart of current educational efforts to educate each child to achieve academic rigorous standards. This moral position springs from the knowledge that prior efforts in public education provided educational rigor for a few and sorted out the rest into a predetermined lower societal class. Moreover, schools overtly participated in establishing and maintaining a tradition of societal elitism and poverty along the lines of race, gender, ethnicity, sexual orientation, religion, and ableism. Ableism, in this text, will be used to mean a "discrimination or prejudice against individuals with disabilities" (Hehir, 2002). As the authors, we understand and acknowledge that educators are the products of our societal context, hence shaped by the education they received. We further understand that without critical self-reflection on the values and beliefs that define our morality, teachers and school leaders are inclined to continue in unquestioning fashion the educational traditions they received.

In this book, we approach cultural proficiency as a moral framework that helps educators respond in ways that educate each child to achieve high academic standards. The path of cultural proficiency is an *inside-out* approach that professes a transformation of values and beliefs that affect the actions of all members of the school community—administrators, counselors, teachers, students, parents, psychologists, custodians, technicians, secretaries, office managers, and so on. The cultural proficiency journey is an examination of what comes *prior* to our outward behaviors—the principles that guide our actions. Traveling this path requires a mind-set and a way of being that esteems the culture of others as you esteem your own culture, while positively engaging, adapting, and responding to each new situation.

In Part I of this book, we describe the framework for understanding cultural proficiency as moral discourse and action. First, we introduce you to Oakland Hills as a setting for case analysis throughout the book. Although a fictional school district, it represents a composite of school systems with which we have worked throughout North America. Second, there is a review of the four tools of cultural proficiency into a conceptual framework that demonstrates the tools as interrelated components. Also in this section, you will find models for discussing morality and the implications for schools.

- Thomas Sergiovanni's (1992) insights on motivation and morality are reviewed as a way of understanding how educators are inspired toward action.
- Jurgen Habermas' (1990) perspective on moral reasoning gives us critical insight into the concept of lifeworld as a backdrop for how we come to understand the world around us.
- Habermas' perspective helps explain why two parties can view an identical event and walk away with two different versions of what transpired. This is particularly important as we venture into proficient dispositions for cross-cultural communications.
- Chris Argyris' (1990) discussion of the Ladder of Inference as presented by Peter Senge (1999) provides a powerful illustration of how a series of inferential steps shape our eventual actions.
- Finally, we discuss Brenda CampbellJones' (2002) model of moral action when performing intentional acts toward social justice.

Part II of this book presents cases for you to apply your understanding of cultural proficiency as a framework for moral action. Each case has thought-provoking dilemmas for critical self-reflection and group discussions. We invite your active participation in probing and understanding the dilemmas presented in each case. The cases are designed to aid your colleagues and you in surfacing personally held assumptions. The dilemmas are to provide an opportunity for your colleagues and you to raise awareness of the role assumptions play in shaping beliefs. Bringing our deeply held *beliefs* (principles) to the surface is fundamental to understanding the actions we take. We encourage you to test your beliefs in light of how well these principles guide you in educating every child and family you serve.

As a staff, we encourage you to read these cases and participate in dialogue using the prompts that accompany each case. The cases can stimulate constructive, culturally proficient ideas and actions for use in your own school setting. Through informed ethical conversations, your colleagues and you cocreate the culturally responsive and responsible reality that serves you and the children in your schools (Gill Monroe, 2006; Lindsey, Roberts, & CampbellJones 2005; Maturana & Varela 1992).

A REWARDINGLY DIFFICULT PROCESS

Read the passage from "Proud Flesh," taken from the article *America for All Americans* and record your response in the spaces provided on the next page.

During my teenage years, I had the wonderful experience of raising horses. Along with the joy of playing with these beautiful animals came the responsibility of caring for them. On occasion, they would develop infectious sores around the hooves of their feet. To prevent a condition of lameness within the animals, the veterinarian would cut deeply in the wound and heavily medicate the area to halt any spreading of infection. Within a short period, a thin layer of tissue known as "proud flesh" would develop over the top of the lacerated area giving the appearance of rapid healing. However, the contrary was the case. This layer acted as a lid providing the perfect caldron for disease to grow and fester, ensuring permanent injury. It was my job to peel away the fleshy layer after it developed and keep the wound clean and properly medicated. Upon removing the flesh, pus would spill from the wound, producing the most awful odor. However, no matter how offensive the smell to my senses, this procedure was necessary to ensure that the wound healed from the inside, preventing a condition of permanent lameness within the animal. As in the case of the injured horses, sometimes we need to dig deeply into wounds that have been covered perhaps too quickly. We need to clean them well no matter how offensive they may initially appear to our senses. We must peel away the "proud flesh" and allow healing to occur from the inside or suffer permanent lameness for the remainder of our years. (Noli & Jones, 1996, pp. 7–22)

What does the "proud flesh" metaphor mean to you? In what ways does it apply to your school? What is your reaction to the metaphor of proud flesh?

_____

_____

_____

_____

Do you think the metaphor is an appropriate picture of the difficulty of the moral work facing educators when it comes to teaching each child to achieve high standards? Why? Why not?

_____

_____

_____

_____

You may have a queasy, unsettled feeling after reading the "Proud Flesh" passage. If so, you are not alone. The thought of digging deeply into an infected wound creates a painful picture. Yet, it is exactly the process necessary for healing that leads to a healthy school environment. Schools have a tradition saturated with unhealthy propagation of systematic oppression and entitlement (Bennett, Jr., 1987; Brown, 1972; Kozol, 1991; Woodson, 1933). Educators will have to dig deeply into the moral under-pinnings that maintain these systemic barriers and purposefully and painfully remove them in order to move forward. Cultural Proficiency is a set of tools designed to move one from unhealthy to healthy values, behav-iors, policies, and practices. The shift engendered in the move from unhealthy to healthy actions has deep moral bases for educators. We are pleased to be on this journey with you.

Acknowledgments

Many people who labor daily to advance full participation of children in our schools inspired this book. For them, educational equity is the critical thread in achieving the American ideal left unfinished by the Founding Fathers—freedom and justice for all citizens. Based upon the original works of Terry Cross (1989), Raymond D. Terrell, Kikanza J. Nuri-Robins, and Randall B. Lindsey are the pioneers who moved the discourse of cultural proficiency into the educational arena in their original works in this subject. They single-handedly expanded the conversations in schools amongst administrators, teachers, counselors, parents, students, and many other members of the school community, allowing schools the opportunity to reinvent themselves within a framework that is responsive to appreciating the culture of others. Their foresight and tireless pursuit inspires a host of scholars, professionals, and laypersons to join in the "movement" of appreciating one another and adapting in ways that move American society toward inclusiveness.

Throughout the United States and Canada, there is growing passion concerning the moral implications for school change. This book addresses cultural proficiency as a moral framework. It is in response to many in the field who rightly question legal and structural issues that impede the educational needs of children. They want to know how they fit into the process of change. We are most appreciative to the many teachers, administrators, counselors, psychologists, social workers, parents, students, secretaries, bus drivers, and custodians who have given us feedback on this critical issue. Their insight has framed much of the content in this book.

We are also deeply thankful to our children and grandchildren who have patiently granted us time away from family to finish this book. Their understanding of our focus and passion and their willingness to grant us the space we needed to finish this volume is sincerely noted. They are the reason we labor intensely on this subject. We further give thanks and appreciation to Delores Lindsey, a lifetime friend and devoted colleague.

A life partner to Randall, her feedback was immeasurable. We give a special thanks as well to John Krownapple for his enthusiastic support and involvement in the conceptualization process of this book. John's knowledge and insight were central in the development of ideas in early stages of this book and are crucial to the evolution of cultural proficiency in schools. We appreciatively thank Shan Boggs and Naomi Renbarger for their tireless editing of our work. Finally, we express sincere thanks to Dan Alpert, our editor, and Megan Bedell, our associate editor. Dan has been a friend throughout this project, providing encouragement and feedback instrumental for completing the book. Megan's assistance with the details of constructing the manuscript proved critical to making its completion a success.

We gratefully acknowledge the contributions of the following reviewers:

Barbara Heuberger Rose
Associate Professor, Department of Teacher Education
Miami University, Oxford, OH

Sarah V. Mackenzie
Assistant Professor, Educational Leadership
University of Maine, Orono, ME

Nate Quinn
Coordinator of Cultural Diversity and Extended Learning
Opportunities
Springfield Public Schools, Springfield, MO

About the Authors

Franklin CampbellJones, EdD, addresses audiences around the world including Thailand, the People's Republic of China, Guam, Canada, and the United States of America. He provides professional learning seminars with schools and districts as they meet the challenges of academic and social needs for *every* student. He has served as high school social science and reading teacher, school administrator, district program director, state director for the California School Leadership Academy, and university professor at California State University, Los Angeles, and Rowan University in Glassboro, New Jersey. He is Vice President of CampbellJones & Associates where he consults with school districts as they apply the tenets of cultural proficiency. He enjoys independent research and scholarship related to organizational change that advances equity in schools and communities. Most of all, he enjoys time with children and grandchildren (www.campbelljones.org).

Brenda CampbellJones, PhD, is formerly an area superintendent of a large urban school district, executive director of one of Azusa Pacific University's regional campuses, and executive director of the California Leadership Academy. President of CampbellJones & Associates, she provides staff development and technical assistance to school districts throughout the United States. Through the lens of cultural proficiency, she coaches and facilitates the change process in school districts that are making systemic changes for academic achievement. Dr. CampbellJones has served students as a teacher, an elementary principal, and an award-winning middle school principal. She brings with her the vision that every child *does* learn and it is up to each of us to meet that opportunity. She thoroughly enjoys time with family and friends (www.campbelljones.org).

Randall B. Lindsey, PhD, is Emeritus Professor, California State University, Los Angeles, and has a practice centered on educational consulting and issues related to diversity. He has served as a teacher, an administrator, executive director of a nonprofit corporation, Interim Dean of Education at California Lutheran University, Distinguished Educator in Residence at Pepperdine University, and Chair of the Education Department at the University of Redlands. All of Randy's experiences have been in working with diverse populations and his area of study is the behavior of white people in multicultural settings. It is his belief and experience that too often white people only observe multicultural issues instead of being personally involved with them. To that end, he designs and implements interventions that address the roles of all sectors of the society.

Randy and his wife (and frequent coauthor), Delores, are enjoying this phase of life as grandparents, educators, and supporters of just causes (randallblindsey@gmail.com).

Part I

Cultural Proficiency and Morality

1 Oakland Hills

I t has been four years since Barbara Campbell left the position of super-intendent of Maple View School District. Her work as a consultant to districts throughout the country is personally rewarding. The joy of helping others nourishes her in ways she had not imagined possible during her climb up leadership ranks in the school system. Today, she carefully reviews files sent to her by Eduardo Soriano, superintendent from a nearby school district. The phone rings. It is Dr. Soriano.

Barbara: Eduardo, I received several files from your office. I am struck by the power of the mission statement.

Eduardo: Yes, it is a powerful mission. We developed it based on the Guiding Principles of Cultural Proficiency. It took a collaborative effort to develop it. It was a real struggle for members of the community, the board, teachers, students, and administrators to pull things together.

Barbara: I can tell from reading that you put a lot of work into the effort to make it happen.

Eduardo: *(Speaking quickly, on edge)* Well, it is a great mission statement. It is something to be proud of, but making it a reality has proven to take a little bit more work than actually crafting the statement.

Barbara: Mmm . . . I see. What seems to be the problem, Eduardo?

Eduardo: It is very difficult to put my finger on just where the problem lies. There seem to be several of them, not just one. One thing is for certain: what we say is our mission is not always consistent with what we do. What we say we want to do seems to be in conflict with what we *actually* do. I do not think we are walking our talk. It is as if we are working against ourselves sometimes. I sent you a file about one of our high schools. I think you will get a flavor of what I mean after you read it.

Barbara: Okay, Eduardo. I have it. I will download it this morning, read it, and then we can discuss it in detail when we meet next week.

After hanging up the phone, Barbara ponders the anxiety in Eduardo's voice. Dr. Soriano had worked his way through the ranks in the Oakland Hills School District. He began his career as a fifth-grade teacher. After five years, he was transferred to the middle school to be the Dean of Students. After a few more years, he became assistant principal, a position he held for six years. His status was eventually elevated to principal, which he served for three years. He was then encouraged by top-level administration to pursue a central-office position, Director of Special Services. He held that position for only two years prior to his current rank as superintendent.

Some in the central-office administration questioned his rapid ascent to the top of the leadership ranks. He had managed to land the top spot of superintendent ahead of two other administrators. Both had worked in the district five years beyond Eduardo's tenure. In fact, they had each held the position of assistant superintendent for two years prior to Eduardo's coming to the central office. Chatter amongst many in the Oakland Hills School District was that either of these two administrators was in line to assume the title of superintendent. The School Board thought otherwise and recruited Eduardo instead. Cautiously, he accepted. Now, he called asking for Barbara's help. He wanted her to perform an audit of the system to inform the district on how well they were progressing toward implementing cultural proficiency. The audit would offer him an objective perspective as to what might be happening in the district.

Barbara knew too well the challenges involved in implementing cultural proficiency systemwide into a school district. She led the charge to make cultural proficiency a high-leverage strategy in the Maple View School District where she was formerly superintendent of schools. After the call ended, Barbara once again looked at Oakland Hills' mission statement.

OAKLAND HILLS SCHOOL DISTRICT MISSION

We strive for personal academic excellence in a safe and caring environment, which allows us to build and value relationships while honoring our cultural and social diversity in a newly developing global community.

We believe . . .

1. Every student learns in an academic culture that allows them to be successful at their own pace and allows educators to build on their strengths.

2. There is a dominant culture and it serves our staff, students, and community in varying degrees.

3. Developing a relationship of trust with students within the dynamics of culture leads to student success.

4. Teaching comes from the heart. The best teachers are called to their profession and all good teachers work as if they are called.

5. Educators must be supported emotionally, academically, and financially as they meet the inherent potential of every student and adapt to their students' changing needs.

6. Educators, school staff, parents, and students contribute to making students feel a part of an important community.

7. For decisions at schools, meeting student needs is the determining factor.

8. Education is not limited to academic settings, but is a valued gift also offered by other institutions or cultural factors as family, spirituality or religion, and community.

9. Public schools will successfully educate every child when people in all social and economic classes are valued in society.

10. Education is a major socializing force in creating an inclusive society that is based on equality of rights, sense of purpose, human dignity, justice, and hope.

Therefore, we will continually:

- Critique and assess the prevailing school culture in order to create culture that serves each student and staff member well.
- Acknowledge individual and group identities and needs within our school and community cultures.
- Recognize the importance of the vast diversity within cultures, as well as acknowledge the diversity that exists between cultures.

"It was a good mission statement," Barbara thought to herself. It had all the qualities needed to foster a culturally competent environment. She reflected upon her experience leading the effort to create a mission statement at her former school district and imagined how things must have been for the Oakland Hills community. They tussled with every word and sentence throughout the entire process. They were careful to embed multiple perspectives from the entire community to capture everyone's values and beliefs. It was a great achievement. It set in motion a vision for providing the best education for each child. But what was going wrong in the Oakland Hills School District? What was the cause of the anxiety in Eduardo Soriano's voice?

Barbara set the mission statement aside. She retrieved an article in the file from the local newspaper, the *Oakland Hills Harbinger.* It was a scathing indictment of one of the district's schools. Titled "Educate or Incarcerate," the article highlighted the divide in the Oakland Hills community along racial lines dating back to court-ordered school desegregation in the 1960s. As local residents resisted school integration, it was a difficult time for the community. African American schools were closed down, forcing children from these communities to attend what were once White-only schools located in White communities. The district bused the children into the schools. Although the event of school integration transpired, social mixing along racial lines was a more difficult achievement. Overt segregationist behaviors transformed into subtle underground practices. Although children attended the same campus occupying the same space, they tended to group themselves along racial lines. This observation was most prevalent in the higher grade levels. In the local high schools, it was common for a White student to attend school and not interact with a single African American student the entire day. In fact, it was possible for that same student to spend his entire high school career without an interracial social experience. The same was true for African American students.

This self-imposed social segregation by students was sanctioned by the school's institutional practices creating student traffic patterns for academic coursework tracked along racial and ethnic lines. Entire floors and wings of the school building were considered Black, White, Latino, or for English Language Learners (ELL) based upon the number of students taking classes in the area. Many Latino and Asian students, particularly newcomers to the school, were placed in the ELL wing specially designed to help them gain language acquisition toward English proficiency. On the other hand, advanced placement and honors classes were primarily attended by White students with a few Asian students and an occasional African American or Latino student in attendance. African American, Latino, Native American and/or First Nation,[1] and Asian students new to the school occupied most remedial courses.

When looking at the Oakland Hills community, the same patterns existed. For all practical purposes, the students followed the lead of their parents. Neighborhoods were segregated as well as religious institutions. This became the way things were in Oakland Hills. Defacto racial segregation was woven into the fabric of the community culture.

However, with the recent boom in housing developments, the old tensions had risen above ground once again. The previously mentioned newspaper article exacerbated the situation. Its central theme pointed to a demographic trend toward increased numbers of residents of color moving into the area. The article raised questions as to whether this change might affect the "standing" of the local schools. Since a great number of Oakland Hills' graduates attended college beyond high school, the article raised doubts as to whether that tradition might continue, given that many "minorities tend" to be incarcerated throughout the country. It cited data showing the high incarceration rate of Blacks and Latinos. "These populations tend to need extra attention so as not to overly use resources in the community," the article concluded.

After the article's appearance, a series of letters and e-mails circulated throughout the community. A letter to the editor written by a long-time resident was printed in the local paper's opinion section, *Voice of the People.*

> *Regarding,* Educate or Incarcerate, *it is clear that things are changing in the Oakland Hills community and they may not always be for the better. Shouldn't we be more concerned about the status of our community? It is my opinion that the long-standing, respected residents of this community should seriously consider how we want to be viewed. It is clear from your article that everyone may not be capable of attending schools at the caliber for which we are accustomed in this community.*
>
> —Grace Richards

The newspaper article also generated a reaction from school employees. A highly influential veteran teacher and president of the teachers union wrote an e-mail to the principal of Pine Hills High School, Dr. Harry Staples. He copied his message to the superintendent. Barbara read the copy from the file.

> Dear Dr. Staples,
>
> I am sure you are aware of the difficulties that we face in maintaining the prominent national academic standing of Pine Hills High School. The school is known throughout the state and indeed the country for its outstanding academic achievements. Many of

our students are national merit scholars, hold the highest scores on college placement exams, and attend the best colleges and universities this country has to offer. Our alumni are university professors, corporate executives, medical doctors, prominent lawyers, and outstanding citizens in the community.

The teachers at Pine Hills High have worked very hard to make sure students achieve at the highest level possible. It is our responsibility to make sure that we cultivate their innate abilities and give them the opportunity to achieve rigorous academics provided they are willing to put forth the effort to be successful.

We are keenly aware that children have different learning aptitudes and that it is our duty to help them live up to their potential. Hence, we are deeply concerned about the proper readiness of the children entering our classrooms. Therefore, we call on you to consider appropriate programs that might assist students at the proper levels, so they have a degree of "readiness" upon their arrival at Pine Hills High.

Sincerely,
Tom Pratt

THE OAKLAND HILLS COMMUNITY

Oakland Hills is a rapidly expanding community nestled at the base of the foothills. The community population has spiraled upward 8% each year for the last 10 years. In a short amount of time, the population grew from 30,000 residents to 64,000. Census data show population distribution as 40% European American, 15% African American, 25% Latino, 15% Asian, 3% Pacific Islander, and 2% Native American. Middle-class residents comprise approximately 70% of the population and are essentially the economic base of the community. Approximately 18% are low salaried with 7% considered to be of the "working" poor. The remaining 5% are of the upper class. A major state highway divides the community creating a clear separation of Eastside and Westside.

Ten years ago, the newly built Pine Hills Estates was completing its first phase of construction for "executive" homes. Located on the Westside of the community, the development is now complete, with more than 300 homes nestled around the exclusive Pine Hills Golf Course. Additional Westside housing developments include Pine Hills Terrace, located just north of the Pine Hills Golf Course and featuring upscale single-family town homes designed with "the professional" in mind. Westside development also includes Waverly Hills and Snowberry Meadows, which target middle-income residents. These developments provide housing for many of the new employees of the Oakland Hills School District.

Added to the growth of established communities in Oakland Hills, a new housing development, South East Hills, has created an influx of middle-class residents. Although the homes are more affordable in the Eastside than the Westside community, the residents identify with members of the Westside. In spite of failing to pass the proposal for affordable housing for the Westside, the Economic Development Subcommittee managed to successfully pass and fund a similar project for the Eastside community. The plan includes a 180-unit apartment complex. Although it met with major resistance from members of the South East Hills community, the proposal passed with a 5–0 vote by the county governing council. A similar proposal was floated for the Westside, but stalled in the subcommittee. Eventually, it was removed from the agenda.

The old downtown has gone through revitalization. Young entre-preneurs moved into the area and created a garden district showcasing fine wines, cafés, coffee houses, bookstores, and music shops. What were once old grain and feed buildings now house attractions for an expanding college-aged population. Tri City Community College, in conjunction with a state university, established a satellite campus two blocks off Main Street.

OAKLAND HILLS SCHOOLS

Over the years, the Oakland Hills Public School system has maintained a reputation of greatness. The school system has consistently scored in the top 8% throughout the state on standardized testing. One of its six high schools, Pine Hills, has recently been ranked 100th nationally among high-achieving schools. In fact, many of the new residents moving to the area said they chose the Oakland Hills community because of the "excel-lent" schools in the district. Many families "fled" other nearby school districts voicing that they were not good for kids. Even in a down mar-ket, some parents sold their homes for the opportunity to have their children attend the Oakland Hills School District. "I only want the best for my child. If selling our home is what it takes for our children to have a good education, then that's what we will do," a resident stated in the local newspaper.

The Oakland Hills School District serves 24,900 students from preschool through Grade 12. The ethnic composition mirrors that of the Oakland Hills community:

African American   20%

Asian American   10%

European American   55%

Latino   10%

Native American and/or First Nation   3%

Pacific Islander   2%

OAKLAND HILLS DILEMMA AS EMBLEMATIC

Barbara's investigation of the Oakland Hills School District gives you the sense of why Eduardo's voice had a tone of urgency as he spoke about implementing cultural proficiency systemwide. Clearly, the Oakland Hills schools face a dilemma. How are they to serve *every* child to meet high academic standards when they have a tradition of serving a few (NAEP, 2007)? This question presents other entanglements that must be carefully unraveled:

1. Does *every* mean *each?*

2. What will happen to the existing hierarchy on campus and in the community when rigorous education is given to each student regardless of gender, race, socioeconomic status, religion, sexual orientation, or ethnicity?

3. Do parents want each student to be well educated or is their interest only in *their* child being the better educated?

4. How would staff positions change? Who gets to teach advanced placement and honors college preparation courses? Will these courses be for everyone? Does every teacher possess the knowledge and skills to teach courses of this "caliber" to all students? Should they be required to teach at these levels?

These are not purely academic questions. The quality of education one receives affects individual success and, indeed, that of a group in society. The response to each question has far-reaching implications that determine fundamentals in society, such as how wealth is distributed; who gets what job; how communities are formed; how families are structured; who shapes political policy, legislative oversight, and law enforcement; and who teaches the next generation.

The Oakland Hills School District typifies the experience of many public-school systems in the United States. They are strapped within a tradition of inequity reflecting a history of bias, discrimination, and disproportion against many groups for the benefits of others. Public schools were not designed in the first place to educate all children to achieve at high academic standards (Spring, 2000). In fact, most schools are structured to sort students along academic and vocational tracks. Beginning in the early years, students in these schools are labeled "below grade-level," "proficient," or "advanced." In some cases, entire schools and communities are grouped according to these designations. For some educators, a student's success in school is more closely related to street address or postal code, rather than academic performance. These groupings determine the quality of educational rigor they will receive throughout their educational experience.

The shift from educating *some* students to educating *each* is paradigmatic. What this suggests is that all of the rules and regulations governing how we view and function in the old paradigm—*some*—will not necessarily apply to the new paradigm—*each*. When a shift of this kind occurs in any organization, in this case schools, the organization has to start from zero to redefine itself to function effectively in the new paradigm (Barker, 2001). The successful organization will begin that journey with a fundamental critique of its purpose relative to its values and beliefs.

In this book, we argue that cultural proficiency is the framework that successfully guides school systems in the journey of redefinition that provides equitable education for each child. Cultural proficiency is an *inside-out* approach to change, where the individual and the organization intentionally engage in transformational processes to effect change. Moreover, applying this approach requires school-system members to critically reflect on the moral underpinnings of school and address, the structures and practices for which these moral foundations support.

Throughout this book, we introduce you to the conceptual framework of cultural proficiency. A description of the conceptual design and its components serves to enhance your understanding of the application of this framework for profound change in schools. We also introduce you to other theoretical frameworks that deepen your understanding of morality and the implications of how ethics govern practices and polices in schools. Interwoven throughout the book are case dilemmas based upon the unfolding Oakland Hills story. Each case has reflective exercises prompting your response for greater comprehension of the framework. All characters, city locations, and schools mentioned in the cases are fictional. However, the cases are based upon actual events.

In the next chapter, you will review the conceptual framework of cultural proficiency highlighting each tool. Before proceeding, review the following questions prepared for the Oakland Hills School District. Think of how you might respond to each one when reviewing your own school. The questions below are organized under the headings of the *Barriers to Cultural Proficiency*. Here, we present them with a brief description, but discuss them in detail later in the book. Each barrier highlights the historical and present-day struggle to advance equity in schools.

- Resistance to Change—Views change as needing to be done by others, not by one's self.
  - How do the educators view their children and families? Do they describe the children as insiders or outsiders? For example, do they use pronouns such as "those" to describe children and families, viewing them as outsiders? Do educators use pronouns such as "our" to create an atmosphere of inclusion when describing students, families, and communities?
  - Do educators critique their values and beliefs when addressing the needs of children and families?

- Systems of Oppression—Acknowledges and recognizes that racism, sexism, ethnocentrism, and other forms of oppression are real experiences.
  - What practices are in the schools that reinforce these barriers? Does the school forcibly track certain students into nonacademic courses? Are new, inexperienced teachers, with the lowest skill levels, assigned to teach students with the greatest needs?
  - What policies are in place at the school or system level that encourage or support these barriers?
  - What artifacts exist that indicate that these barriers are in place, e.g., student achievement gaps between demographic groups, inequitable proportionality of student demographic groups in college preparatory courses, etc.?
  - What beliefs are present that maintain and propagate these systems? For instance, "I believe that children have innate learning abilities that will allow them to experience certain levels of learning. Some have it and some don't."

- A Sense of Privilege and Entitlement—Unawareness of indifference to benefits that accrue solely by one's membership in a gender, race, or other cultural group.

○ Are there practices or policies in place that serve one group better than another? Do veteran teachers get their choice of students? Are certain families served better than others?
○ Do some groups purposefully have unfair advantages over others? What beliefs support these practices?
○ Do new teachers get the least support? Are they forced to move from room to room due to space issues, while veteran teachers stay in a single room? What are the underlying values that support this practice?

Reflection

What questions resonate with you when reading the list above?

_____

_____

_____

_____

How do these questions relate to your school or district?

_____

_____

_____

_____

What other questions come to mind when reading the Oakland Hills School District case?

_____

_____

_____

_____

NOTE

1.   A collective and emerging term that describes indigenous people who are not Inuit or Metis—Province of Ontario, Canada. *Human rights code.*

2 The Tools of Cultural Proficiency

Justice is what love looks like when it is said in public.

—Michael Eric Dyson (2008)

GETTING CENTERED

The situations described below occur all too frequently in our schools. While reading them, be fully aware of your feelings and reactions:

- You read reports of the very high levels of high school dropout rates in which young people who are African American, Latino, Native American and/or First Nations and who are from families of low income are vastly overrepresented.
- You overhear bigoted comments about students from your colleagues.
- Students in your school make bigoted, insensitive comments to one another.
- You attend a professional development seminar or a university course, and the presenter appears to minimize issues of diversity and equity.

How do you react to these statements? What did you say and feel at the time you may have witnessed or experienced these occurrences? What do you *wish* you had said at the time? Take a few moments to recall your reactions and feelings. What words come to mind as you think of the statements and the people

(Continued)

(Continued)

who uttered them? Be mindful not to describe the person or the event. Just focus on you and your reaction. You may be recalling your reaction at the time. You may be aware that older, past feelings re-emerge for you. You may even be reacting to the fact that you did not respond at the time of the original occurrence. Whatever your responses, use this space to record your thoughts and feelings:

_____

_____

_____

_____

MORAL CONSCIOUSNESS

Look back over the comments you wrote above. Most likely, you had feelings and reactions described with words such as *right, wrong, ought,* or *should.* You may have used words and phrases such as *it was not just* or *it is so unfair.* Having feelings and reactions such as these are indicative of people who are conscious of the existence of morality as integral to who they are.

In the upcoming chapters of this book, we introduce you to the work of Chris Argyris (1990), Jürgen Habermas (1990), Thomas Sergiovanni (1992), and Brenda CampbellJones (2002), as a means to exploring the moral and ethical underpinning for your own personal and professional behavior. This will enable you to influence the culture of your school. The previous activity, and the major purposes of this book, are to provide you with the direction and tools to negotiate ethical barriers that *inhibit* educational practices embedded within the culture of your school and to create awareness that can lead to conditions for profound school change.

Profound school change is an organic, nonlinear process comprised of two overlapping and interactive phases:

- The recognition or development of a moral consciousness for doing what is right.
- An ethical framework of moral principles to guide one's behavior.

CULTURAL PROFICIENCY IS A MORAL CONSCIOUSNESS PROCESS

Cross (1989) describes cultural proficiency as being an "inside-out process" of personal and organizational change. Fundamentally, this means that sustainable change occurs in the intersubjective world and crystallizes in the objective. What we value and believe gives rise to the actions and behaviors that we see. In other words, we project our internal vision onto the outer world around us to make sense of what we observe (Zohar, 1990).

Dr. Martin Luther King, Jr. (1998) stated, "Humankind has advanced technologically to conquer outer space, but humankind has not had the moral commitment to conquer their inner space." From King's perspective, our technical advancements will eventually be squandered in light of our unwillingness to overcome inconsistencies in our morality.[1] Cultural proficiency is a lens through which we explore and expand our moral views. The Guiding Principles of Cultural Proficiency inform what we consider to be right or just, which then guides our personal behaviors, organizational policies, and practices. Cultural proficiency involves recognizing who we are as moral beings and our commitment to doing what is right and just, even in the face of overwhelming odds and criticism. Using cultural proficiency as an inside-out process, we become students of our assumptions about self, others, and the context in which we work with others. Therefore, the changes we need to make are from the inside-out.

Tools of Cultural Proficiency: Moral Consciousness and Apparatus

In your response to the questions at the beginning of this chapter, you recorded reactions and feelings. Most likely, they can be classified as *right* vs. *wrong* and issues of what is *fair* or *just* and expressed how things *ought* or *should be*. Responses of this nature are an expression of morality—a compass point for appropriate action. The tools of cultural proficiency are actionable means to identify right from wrong in serving the needs of historically underserved students within the context of serving the needs of all students. Through this approach, historically underserved students gain access to educational opportunities that result in high academic achievement. Furthermore, when education is delivered in a culturally proficient manner all students understand and value the culture with which they identify and the cultures of those around them that may be different from their own.

There are four tools of cultural proficiency to guide the work of schools. These tools make up an interactive, interdependent framework that conceptualizes personal and organizational practice.

- The Guiding Principles of Cultural Proficiency—An inclusive set of core values that identify the centrality of culture in our lives and in our society. These principles provide a philosophical underpinning for educators providing the compass points to inform action in a culturally competent manner.
- Barriers to Cultural Proficiency—The recognition that systems of historical oppression continue to exist, and, in many cases, keep broad-based school reform from equitably educating historically underrepresented groups. These barriers can be overcome by people and organizations that adapt their values, behaviors, policies, and practices to meet the needs of underserved cultural groups through democratic means.
- The Cultural Proficiency Continuum—Six points along a continuum to indicate ways of responding to cultural difference. The continuum uses language, such as "healthy" or "unhealthy," to describe policies and practices used by educators.
- The Essential Elements of Cultural Competence—Five standards to guide a person's values and behaviors and a school/district's policies and practices in meeting the needs of cultural groups.

Tables 2.1 through 2.5 provide an orientation and overview of cultural proficiency. In the chapters that follow, these tools are integrated with communication techniques for your personal work. They are useful for working with colleagues, as you continue to improve your practice in service and support of diverse cultures in schools and communities.

THE GUIDING PRINCIPLES: MORAL FOUNDATION

The cultural proficiency principles provide educators the foundation for moral judgment. It is critical that you adopt these principles as a foundation for moral reasoning to guide the work done in schools on behalf of children and their families. We posit that not adopting these principles makes the pursuit of cultural proficiency difficult, if not impossible. Table 2.1

provides a brief description of each principle taken from the literature (Lindsey, Nuri-Robins, & Terrell, 2003; Nuri-Robins, Lindsey R., Lindsey D., & Terrell, 2006; and Lindsey, Roberts, & CampbellJones, 2005). As you read each one, consider how it applies to your philosophical worldview.

Table 2.1 Guiding Principles of Cultural Proficiency
1. *Culture Is a Predominant Force.* Acknowledge culture as a predominant force in shaping behaviors, values, and institutions. Although you may be inclined to take offense at behaviors that differ from yours, remind yourself that it may not be personal; it may be cultural.
2. *People Are Served in Varying Degrees by the Dominant Culture.* What works well in organizations and in the community for you and others who are like you may work against members of other cultural groups. Failure to make such an acknowledgment puts the burden for change on one group.
3. *The Group Identity of Individuals Is as Important as Their Individual Identities.* Although it is important to treat all people as individuals, it is also important to acknowledge the group identity of individuals. Actions must be taken with the awareness that the dignity of a person is not guaranteed unless the dignity of his or her people is also preserved.
4. *Diversity Within Cultures Is Vast and Significant.* Since diversity within cultures is as important as diversity between cultures, it is important to learn about cultural groups not as monoliths, for example Asians, Latinos, Gay Men, and Women, but as the complex and diverse groups that they are. Often, because of the class differences in the United States, there will be more in common across cultural lines than within them.
5. *Each Group Has Unique Cultural Needs.* Each cultural group has unique needs that cannot be met within the boundaries of the dominant culture. Expressions of one group's cultural identity do not imply disrespect for yours. Make room in your organization for several paths that lead to the same goal.
6. *The Best of Both Worlds Enhances the Capacity of All.* When people adopt the practices of other cultures that improve their ability to communicate and problem solve cross-culturally, they are more effective both for themselves and for those with whom they work.

The Guiding Principles of Cultural Proficiency provide an inclusive worldview that embraces Freire's (1987) maxim that there is "no teaching without learning" (p. 56). Together, they give a structure to examine biannual reports, such as National Association of Educational Progress (NAEP), to conclude that current educational practices are not equitable. Accordingly, we recognize that some students are well served by current policies and practices. Unfortunately, those served well may fall prey to a sense of entitlement and privilege that causes them to turn a blind eye to those not well served. It is this dynamic tension between who is well served and who is underserved that leads us into dialogue. Embracing the Guiding Principles of Cultural Proficiency provides a framework for ensuring a successful dialogue, enabling us to serve better the educational needs of each student.

Kohlberg (1973), Gilligan (1983), Argyris (1990), Habermas (1990), Sergiovanni (1992), and CampbellJones (2002), each describe individuals with a highly evolved sense of moral purpose. They describe individuals with a sense of justice and fairness who transcend prevailing norms with the intent to serve the underserved. It is these evolved senses of justice and fairness that lead to using the Guiding Principles of Cultural Proficiency as ethical maxims to overcome barriers to proficiency and achieve profound school change.

BARRIERS TO CULTURAL PROFICIENCY

The barriers to cultural proficiency are recognizable systems of historical oppression that continue to exist in the policies and practices of schools. As we will see in the section that follows, they are aligned with the left side of the Cultural Proficiency Continuum. They manifest in three distinct ways:

- Resistance to Change—Viewing change as needing to be done by others, not by one's self.
- Systems of Oppression—Acknowledging and recognizing that racism, sexism, ethnocentrism, and other forms of oppression are real experiences.
- A Sense of Privilege and Entitlement—A sense of privilege and entitlement arises from indifference to benefits that accrue solely by one's membership in a gender, race, or other cultural group. This barrier encapsulates the practice of denying one group societal benefits, while awarding those same benefits to others.

The barriers represent the intractable issues that have historically, as well as presently, stymied broad-scale school reform intended to provide adequate and appropriate education to historically underserved cultural groups of students. The resistance to change by educators is embodied in two highly observable ways. First, every two years since 1971, the NAEP (Perie, Moran, & Lutkus, 2005) has documented, and circulated widely in the education community, detailed descriptions of academic achievement gaps. NAEP data highlight these persistent disparities as a pattern of continuous underservice for historically underrepresented groups by schools. Second, in spite of the NAEP data being very public, it has taken state and national education reforms, most widely evident in the federal reauthorization of Elementary and Secondary Education Act (ESEA) Title I's No

Child Left Behind Act (2001), to set targets for academic achievement in order to hold educators accountable. The continuing presence of educational gaps is a challenge to those of us at all levels in the education community, requiring us to examine why educational and academic achievement gaps continue to persist among certain demographic groups of our students. These gaps are evidence of accrued benefits for some and lack thereof for others, passed from one generation to the next. As a profession, educators struggle to address the inequities seen in the well-documented data. Many educators, however, act as if the NAEP data does not exist. Making visible and addressing equity issues previously ignored is at the heart of cultural proficiency.

THE CULTURAL PROFICIENCY CONTINUUM

The Cultural Proficiency Continuum (Table 2.2) gives language to describe healthy and unhealthy states of being for individuals and organizations. It is a template for describing the *behaviors* of educators and the *practices* of schools. With it, you have a way of explaining your values and beliefs associated with actions that manifest in your practices. There are six points on the continuum:

- Cultural Destructiveness: See the difference and stomp it out.
- Cultural Incapacity: See the difference and make it wrong.
- Cultural Blindness: See the difference and act like you don't see it.
- Cultural Precompetence: See the difference and respond to it inappropriately.
- Cultural Competence: See the difference that difference makes.
- Cultural Proficiency: See the difference, respond positively, engage, adapt, and commit to social justice.

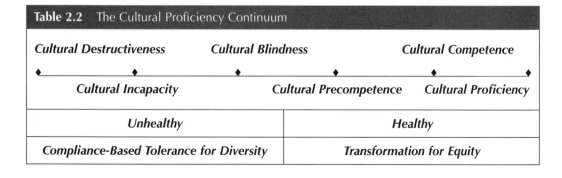

Table 2.2 The Cultural Proficiency Continuum

Cultural Destructiveness	*Cultural Blindness*	*Cultural Competence*
◆————————◆————————◆————————◆————————◆————————◆		
Cultural Incapacity	*Cultural Precompetence*	*Cultural Proficiency*
Unhealthy	*Healthy*	
Compliance-Based Tolerance for Diversity	*Transformation for Equity*	

SOURCE: Adapted from Raymond D. Terrell and Randall B. Lindsey. (2009). *Culturally Proficient Leadership: The Personal Journey Begins Within.* Thousand Oaks, CA: Corwin.

Table 2.3 elaborates on the continuum by including language and behaviors that characterize each point. Note the actions associated with each point. Behaviors and practices located on the left side of the continuum—destructiveness, incapacity, blindness—give evidence of barriers to cultural proficiency. Behaviors and practices on the right side of the continuum—precompetence, competence, proficiency—specifically those regarded as culturally competent and proficient—reflect commitment to the guiding principles as educators' and schools' moral bearing and reliance on the guiding principles as ethical assumptions.

The Cultural Proficiency Continuum allows you to move from *unhealthy* points, associated on the left side, toward those that are associated with *healthy* points on the right side. Beliefs associated with the left side of the continuum hold a perspective that sees children's cultural attributes as negative, or even as contaminants to the school's environment. This results in educators describing children in destructive or incapacitating ways. For example, you might refer to children by their postal zip code, thereby tagging them as coming from undesirable neighborhoods. Comments such as *If we could only get rid of those trailer-park kids our scores would be higher* are common associations with the left side of the continuum. Even further, at the point of cultural blindness, you might view children's culture as nonexistent and simply not recognize it as a contributing factor to what makes the school a school. For example, it is common for teachers to proclaim they do not see color in children. What this communicates to children of color is that their experience, in a racialized society, is to be discounted.

However, the opposite is true for points of view conceived on the right side of the continuum. It is from the vantage points of precompetence, competence, and proficiency that you come to accept culture as a viable force and begin to witness diversity as a natural condition of interdependence in healthy societies (Maturana & Varela, 1992). The actions consistent with the right side of the continuum esteem the culture of the children and their families, advocate and commit to social justice, and create an environment of mutual respect as a way of life. The opposite of the proclamation of not seeing color in children is to acknowledge color as a biological feature of the human experience and appreciate it as genius in human evolution (http://www.pbs.org/race/images/race-guide-lores.pdf; CampbellJones, B. & CampbellJones, F., 2002).

Table 2.4 on page 25 highlights the unhealthy and healthy perspectives associated with the left and right side of the cultural proficiency continuum. Displayed is a fundamental shift in perspective, between the left and right sides of the continuum that comes about when adopting the principles of cultural proficiency as core beliefs and the

Table 2.3 The Cultural Proficiency Continuum: Description and Action

Point on the Continuum	Description	Action	Associated Language
Cultural Destructiveness: See the difference and stomp it out.	Language and behavior at this point disparage, negate, or purge cultures that are different from your own.	Examples are genocide, ethnocide, eliminating historical accounts of cultures from school curriculum, eliminating societal contributions of groups other than the dominant culture including contributions in mathematics, science, art, and civics.	If we could only get rid of those special education students, we would make adequate yearly progress (AYP). Why do we have to celebrate Jewish holidays? Let's just celebrate the *normal* ones.
Cultural Incapacity: See the difference and make it wrong. Elevate the superiority of your own cultural values and beliefs and suppress cultures that are different from your own.	Descriptive language at this point characterizes nondominant groups as less important than the dominant culture.	Includes lowered expectations for student groups, parents, and communities who are not or cannot be assimilated into the dominant culture.	In my class, I group my kids as blue birds, red birds, and buzzards. What do you expect from those kids, they come from parents who don't care. John can't be on the diversity committee. He's White.
Cultural Blindness: See the difference and act like you don't. A state of cultural denial. Act as if differences among cultures do not exist and/or refuse to recognize any differences.	The assumption at this point is that society is a meritocracy and that current and/or historical disparities between groups have been eliminated or never existed.	Proclamations of not seeing color in children or treating all children the same are commonplace.	I don't see color in my kids. I see them as all the same. It isn't fair to the others if we differentiate instruction. They should try harder.
Cultural Precompetence: See the difference and respond inappropriately. Recognize that lack of knowledge, experience, and understanding of other cultures limits your ability to effectively interact with students.	Precompetent awareness signifies engagement in risk-taking behaviors aimed at dismantling the barriers of entitlement and nonadaptation. However, the responses are typically nonsystemic and haphazard, often requiring little or no change in regular school or classroom operations to meet the cultural needs of students.	Examples include quick fixes and short-term programs, delegation of diversity work to those who have been historically underserved or disenfranchised, and acknowledging culture superficially through events such as Black History Month, Women's History Month, Cinco De Mayo, etc.	We had a great multi-cultural festival. We do it once every year. Let's have Su Ling start an Asian parent group. She's Asian, isn't she?

(Continued)

Table 2.3 (Continued)

Point on the Continuum	Description	Action	Associated Language
Cultural Competence: See the difference that difference makes. The essential elements of cultural proficiency are at this point of the continuum. This point meets standards (doing what we are supposed to do).	Competent behaviors include ongoing self-education and respectful responses to others while using the tools of cultural proficiency. Interact with other cultural groups in ways that recognize and value their differences and motivate you to assess your own skills, expand your knowledge and resources, and ultimately cause you to adapt your relational behavior.	Actions include regular opportunities for students to contribute their knowledge, abilities, and perspectives in a variety of ways. Such knowledge about students is used to plan, sequence, and adapt lessons, curriculum, and pedagogical practices. Examples include: reflecting before and/or after conducting a classroom lesson upon such questions as the following: Who is served well by this lesson? Who is not being served well by this lesson? How can I reteach this lesson to bring students not served well to the center of this lesson? Strategies ensure that students' successes are articulated vertically and horizontally across grade levels, departments within schools, and between feeder schools.	I see you are frustrated teaching our new Muslim students. Your frustration hasn't been my experience. May I share? My new neighbors are from Mexico. I am learning Spanish as they are learning English so that we can communicate better. I adapted my curriculum and instruction to bridge the relationship gap between the gay and lesbian students and the heterosexual students in my class. Achievement and discipline has improved tremendously.
Cultural Proficiency: See the difference, respond positively, engage, adapt, commit, and take action for social justice. Honor the differences among cultures, seeing diversity as a benefit. Engage all stakeholders with other cultures to close gaps in order to achieve equitable outcomes and social justice for every cultural group.	Cultural proficiency entails an ever-evolving journey where one engages with and esteems the culture of another. Central is the acknowledgment of interdependence and interacting knowledgeably and respectfully among a variety of cultural groups. One seeks alliances with individuals and groups unlike their own leading to personal and organizational transformation.	Examples include: transformation of curriculum and pedagogical practices that place students' cultural attributes at the center of classroom learning. Promotes and integrates social justice and multiple perspectives into curriculum and instruction. Models, advocates, and encourages staff and students in continuing opportunities to *learn how to learn*—develops academic ability, intellectual competence, and advocacy for social justice.	I have integrated social justice issues into my math curriculum as well as transformed the curriculum to reflect the variety of cultural groups in my class. Next year, I will change to reflect the new cultural groups entering my class. I have adapted my curriculum and instruction to bridge cultural gaps amongst and between students and myself.

SOURCE: Adapted from *Cultural Proficiency: A Manual for School Leaders* (2nd ed; pp. 85–91), by R. B. Lindsey, K. Nuri-Robins, and R. D. Terrell, 2003, Thousand Oaks, CA: Corwin. Copyright © Lindsey, Robins, Terrell.

Table 2.4 Cultural Proficiency Continuum Shift in Perspective

Perspective	Unhealthy Perspective	Orientation in Perspective	Healthy Perspective
Barriers to Cultural Proficiency	*Cultural Destructiveness, Incapacity, and Blindness*	*Shifts in Perspective* *Ethical Disequilibrium*	*Cultural Precompetence, Competence, and Proficiency*
Systems of Oppression: Acknowledging, participating in, and maintaining racism, sexism, ethnocentrism, and other forms of oppression of groups.	• Dominance of others • See others as a liability • Low expectation of others • Ignores cultural assets of others	*Adopt the Principles of Cultural Proficiency* *Use Essential Elements as Standards of Action*	• Reciprocal relationships • Sees others as an asset • High expectation of others • Mutually esteem culture for self and others
Resistance to Change: Viewing change as needing to be done by others, not by one's self.	• Focuses on others to change • Intolerant of change • Sees change as imposition		• Focuses on personal and organizational change • Embraces change • Sees change as a constant
A Sense of Privilege and Entitlement: Unawareness of indifference to benefits that accrue solely by one's membership in a gender, racial, or other cultural group.	• I deserve it because of who I am, because of the cultural group to which I belong • It is my prerogative to act or choose. Power is centralized in me • I have the right to claim it regardless of others		• I seek mutual benefits for others as well as myself • Shared decision making and equitable power distribution • Equitable claim to resources and benefits

use of the essential elements as standards of action. In addition, disequilibrium arises due to the struggle to disengage with past actions associated with unhealthy perspectives tied to the barriers and a subsequent move toward a healthy perspective connected to the Guiding Principles. You become balanced and congruent when healthy behaviors described in the essential elements evolve from the guiding principles of cultural proficiency.

Our word of encouragement is to anticipate disorientation and *move through it*. Many on the journey of cultural proficiency report feelings of emotional disturbance or discomfort when moving from cultural blindness to precompetence on the continuum. In fact, some have stated, "It was easier when I was blind to the situation rather than to now be aware of it." Accepting that this shift in perspective comes with a moment of disturbance makes meeting the standard of cultural competence possible.

Reflection Activity

Now that you have studied the continuum and the barriers, what are your thoughts and reactions?

_____

_____

_____

_____

Where do you see yourself relative to the students in your school?

_____

_____

_____

_____

Where do you see your school along the continuum?

_____

_____

_____

_____

List practices in your school at each point of the continuum.

Destructive   Precompetence

●————————————————————————————————●

_____

_____

Incapacity   Competence

●————————————————————————————————●

_____

_____

Blindness   Proficiency

●————————————————————————————————●

_____

_____

The continuum makes clear the moral angle for educating all students to high levels in preparing them to be responsible in a changing, diverse world. Most educators want their educational practice aligned with the right side of the continuum. However, they most likely do not understand how to make this alignment happen and may not have the resolve to ask the difficult, critical questions of *why not?* Our discussion in later chapters of the Ladder of Inference (Argyris, 1990), motivation (Sergiovanni, 1992), and intentional moral action (CampbellJones, 2002) will assist you in framing a dialogue with your colleagues and can make it possible to address issues of *why not?* Furthermore, our discussion of how this is a moral rather than technical issue will help deepen the dialogue (Delpit, 1995; Fullan, 2003; Habermas, 1990; Kohlberg, 1973).

THE ESSENTIAL ELEMENTS

Once you have acknowledged the Barriers to Cultural Proficiency, adopted the Guiding Principles of Cultural Proficiency, and utilized the Cultural Proficiency Continuum to frame conversations in your work setting, you are ready to employ the Five Essential Elements as standards. When this occurs, you are able to ask difficult questions of yourself and colleagues. These five elements become the standards by which schools measure the efficacy of curriculum, the effectiveness of instructional strategies, the relevance of professional development, the utility of systems of assessment and accountability, and the intent of parent and community communications and outreach.

The Five Essential Elements exist at the "cultural competence" point of the continuum. This point on the continuum meets standards (doing what we are supposed to be doing). Competency is when an educator or school has incorporated the essential elements into their practice to the extent that they develop at least these five commitments:

- A commitment to social justice that addresses the educational needs of every current and emerging cultural group in the school and community.
- A commitment to advocacy that is natural, normal, and effective.
- A commitment to mentoring the historically underserved and to give them educational opportunities that allow them to thrive academically and socially.
- A commitment to mentoring those historically well served by current practice to become aware of and responsive to those historically underserved individuals and cultural groups.
- A commitment to leveling the playing field so every cultural group can participate as colleagues, students, and/or members of the community.

Table 2.5 contains concise descriptions of the Five Essential Elements.

Each element contains empowering language of learning and serves as a standard for professional behavior and schoolwide practices.

Table 2.5 The Essential Elements for Culturally Proficient Practices
• Assessing Cultural Knowledge—Learning about one's own culture, others' cultures, how the school as a whole react to others' cultures, and what you need to do to be effective in cross-cultural situations. Also, leading for learning about the school and its grade levels and departments as cultural entities.

- Valuing Diversity—Creating informal and formal decision-making groups inclusive of people whose viewpoints and experiences are different from yours—and the school's dominant group—that will enrich conversations, decision making, and problem solving.

- Managing the Dynamics of Difference—Modeling problem solving and conflict resolution strategies as a natural and normal process within the culture of the schools and the cultural contexts of the communities of your school.

- Adapting to Diversity—Learning about cultural groups different from your own and the ability to use others' cultural experiences and backgrounds in all school settings.

- Institutionalizing Cultural Knowledge—Making learning about cultural groups and their experiences and perspectives an integral part of the school's professional development.

SOURCE: Adapted from Raymond D. Terrell and Randall B. Lindsey. (2009). *Culturally Proficient Leadership: The Personal Journey Begins Within*. Thousand Oaks, CA: Corwin.

Reflection

Thus far, you have been on quite a tour. You have proceeded from a description of the Guiding Principles, the Barriers to Proficiency, and the Cultural Proficiency Continuum, and have now arrived at a consideration of the five standards intended to support you in service of each student in your classroom and school. How do you react to the Essential Elements? In what way do the Essential Elements reflect the ethics—the values and beliefs—in the Guiding Principles of Cultural Proficiency? To what extent do you want these standards to serve your educational practice and that of your school? Use the space below to record your responses.

_____

_____

_____

_____

CULTURAL PROFICIENCY CONCEPTUAL FRAMEWORK

What do the tools look like when interacting with one another? Figure 2.1 displays the tools and the manner in which they interact and inform one another. It is best to read the table from the bottom up. Note the placement

Figure 2.1 The Conceptual Framework for Culturally Proficient Practices

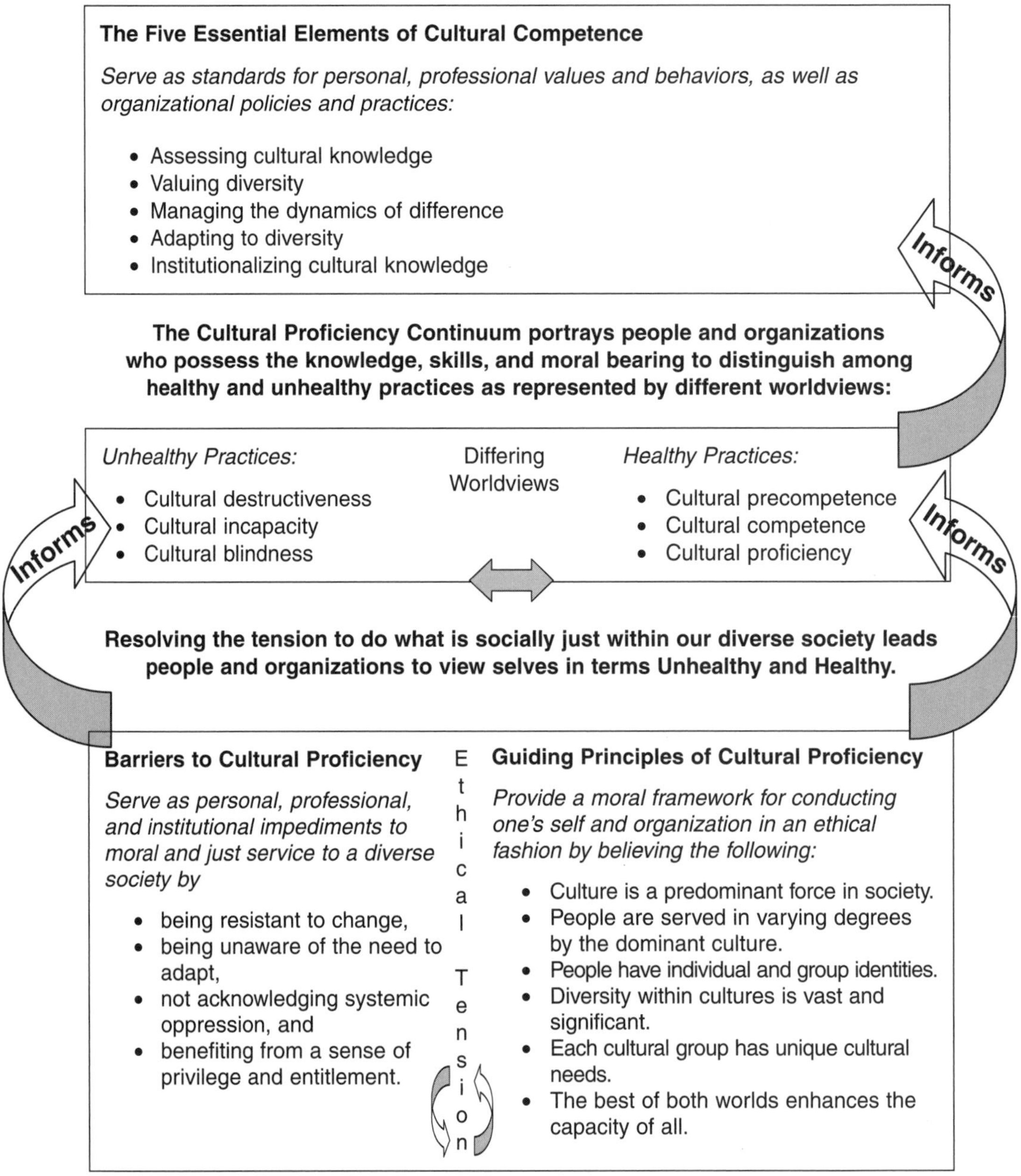

The Five Essential Elements of Cultural Competence

Serve as standards for personal, professional values and behaviors, as well as organizational policies and practices:

- Assessing cultural knowledge
- Valuing diversity
- Managing the dynamics of difference
- Adapting to diversity
- Institutionalizing cultural knowledge

Informs

The Cultural Proficiency Continuum portrays people and organizations who possess the knowledge, skills, and moral bearing to distinguish among healthy and unhealthy practices as represented by different worldviews:

Unhealthy Practices:

- Cultural destructiveness
- Cultural incapacity
- Cultural blindness

Differing Worldviews

Healthy Practices:

- Cultural precompetence
- Cultural competence
- Cultural proficiency

Informs *Informs*

Resolving the tension to do what is socially just within our diverse society leads people and organizations to view selves in terms Unhealthy and Healthy.

Barriers to Cultural Proficiency

Serve as personal, professional, and institutional impediments to moral and just service to a diverse society by

- being resistant to change,
- being unaware of the need to adapt,
- not acknowledging systemic oppression, and
- benefiting from a sense of privilege and entitlement.

Ethical Tension

Guiding Principles of Cultural Proficiency

Provide a moral framework for conducting one's self and organization in an ethical fashion by believing the following:

- Culture is a predominant force in society.
- People are served in varying degrees by the dominant culture.
- People have individual and group identities.
- Diversity within cultures is vast and significant.
- Each cultural group has unique cultural needs.
- The best of both worlds enhances the capacity of all.

of the four tools. First, observe that the barriers that inform the left side of the continuum foster a perspective leading to practices that are culturally destructive, incapacitating, and blinding. Second, observe that the principles that inform the right side of the continuum foster a perspective leading to practices that are culturally precompetent, competent, and proficient.

It is important to note that an ethical tension arises between the Barriers to Cultural Proficiency and the Guiding Principles. As mentioned previously, this tension occurs as a matter of process when adopting the Guiding Principles to inform your worldview. Frequently, educators experience disequilibrium because the philosophical underpinnings of the principles are quite different from the prevailing beliefs that govern schools. For example, Principle 4 states: *Diversity Within Cultures is Vast and Significant.* Since diversity within cultures is as important as diversity between cultures, it is essential to understand that cultural groups are not simply monoliths, for example, Asians, Latinos, gay men, and women. This principle stresses the complex diversification existing within each group. Because of class differences in the United States, there will be more in common across cultural lines than within them. However, for many of us, it seems astonishing that there exists more variation *within* a given group than between groups when in fact *that is the case.* In concrete terms, there is more variation (diversity) within the group labeled "White" than *between* the two groups we label "White" and "African American."

Reflection

Study the conceptual framework of cultural proficiency in Figure 2.1. What resonates with you the most? Record your response in the space provided.

_____

_____

_____

_____

Cultural proficiency takes us on a journey of open engagement in overcoming barriers that perpetuate legacies of oppression. Resistance to changing educational practice is tied to the intractability of the historical systems of oppression such as racism, ethnocentrism, sexism, classism, and heterosexism. Your responses to the reflections in this chapter most likely serve as indicators to levels of comfort in dealing with these issues. Think of your colleagues and imagine how they might respond to the words in Figure 2.1. That is where the dialogue must take place—with and among colleagues. For many people, the words and phrases above will appear scary and/or irritating. Some readers may respond by feeling blamed, angry, guilty, or depressed, and with questions such as *Where do we go from here?* Other readers may respond by feeling validated, or curious, and with questions such as *Yes, so this is my reality and what are we going to do about it?* For them the Barriers to Cultural Proficiency are bleatingly obvious and their expectation is that others should be as aware of the barriers as they are.

A larger question is why are things invisible to some and obvious to others? Further, when we observe social injustice, what keeps us from stopping it? Fundamentally, what makes us resistant to change in the first place? How do we activate ourselves to change and do this differently? The answer to these questions is at the heart of cultural proficiency. In the next chapters, we discuss morality as the compass for our actions. We examine closely several models for understanding values, assumptions, and beliefs relative to observable action.

NOTE

1.   See the discussion of "Lifeworld" in Chapter 4 for a greater understanding of the inside-out process.

3

Values, Assumptions, and Beliefs Guide Our Actions

We do not really see through our eyes or hear through our ears, but through our beliefs.

—Lisa Delpit, 1995

GETTING CENTERED

Think of a time, not in your role as an educator, when you met a person for the first time from a culture different from yours or attended a cultural event that was an unusual experience for you. Do you remember how you studied the person or event? Can you recall the judgments you made? If you had the opportunity to get to know the person or the event, recall your earlier judgments that you later learned to be true and those that were not even close to being true.

_____

_____

_____

_____

In his book *Blink,* Gladwell (2005) makes the point that "snap" decisions are as important as more thoughtfully deliberated ones (p. 15). He contends

(Continued)

(Continued)

that both types of decisions are fraught with assumptions and that understanding those assumptions is important to discovering what we value. Uncovering what we value helps us know how we assign importance. What we view as important over time crystallizes into general principles or beliefs that ultimately dictate our behavior.

A major premise of this book is that our morality—which is comprised of two important aspects, values and beliefs—guides our actions. The aspects that we hold near and dear are the foundation for all that we do. For most of us, deeply woven within the subconscious are values like honesty, respect, and promptness. These aspects of morality function as background mostly taken for granted as we go about our daily routines. They are essential in shaping how we govern our lives as we interact with other human beings (Schein, 2004).

Some argue that real change—change that lasts—happens at this level when we examine what we value and believe (Arygis, 1990; Senge, 1999). To be very serious about changing things to the point of providing a rigorous education for every child, educators have to go beneath the surface level of the usual tinkering with policy, structures, procedures, or resources and critically challenge underlying values, assumptions, and beliefs that shape these cultural aspects of schools. Cultural proficiency holds that the challenge needs to be executed by the holder of the value, assumption, or belief in order for change to be most effective and sustaining—namely, by the educators within the schools. So, what are the ways we can move forward with this examination? We turn to the Ladder of Inference for guidance.

THE LADDER OF INFERENCE

How do we bring these aspects of ourselves to the foreground where we can critically examine them? Making the reasons for our actions visible was at the crux of Chris Argyis's (1990) work. In trying to explain defensive routines practiced by members of corporations leading to behaviors he termed "skilled incompetence," Argyis developed a hypothetical model called the Ladder of Inference. The idea is to illustrate how an individual's observable action might be traced on a series of steps up a ladder. Imagine starting from the bottom rung of a ladder and climbing to the top. You can picture a process within the subjective world that leads to concrete observable action. Peter Senge and colleagues (1994) later expanded Argyis' model to include the seven steps reviewed below.

Rung 1, Observe Data: Located on this rung is all observable data and actual experience, as captured by a device such as a movie camera or digital recorder. Essentially, all data present in a given setting or situation is considered at this rung. As you read this book, around you are mounds of data, such as chair, car, lighting, people, clothing, etc. The list is endless depending on your location and experience. Included in this list is your emotional or physical state, including health, appetite, nourishment, and so on. In a classroom, data might consist of students, facilities, and climate, for example. These are all data to consider at this step on the ladder.

Rung 2, Select Data: This rung represents data you select based upon what you *believe* to be important. This is an important step. It contends that you ignore other data present although it is readily available and simply focus upon what you consider important. Even though there are mounds of data in front of us, these data become invisible once you focus your attention on what you *believe* to be important. (We discuss more about invisibility in Rung 6.) For example, your focus on student achievement might consist of a student's social economic status, racial classification, gender, and so on.

Rung 3, Add Cultural Meaning: You add cultural meaning as a process of interpreting selected data. It is here that your cultural experience fully engages and you assign importance and appreciation to the data based upon your socialized experience. Terms like good, bad, wonderful, and respect, to name a few, highlight this rung. For example, you not only have a student in your class, you have a "good student." The list of cultural value characterizations is not comprehensive. Later in this chapter you will complete an exercise to help identify prevailing values that operate in your life.

Rung 4, Make Assumptions: You form assumptions based on the value placed on the data. Assumptions are guesses you make about what direction to take given the data you selected. For example, if a value you hold is an appreciation for knowledge, then you might assume that the work you do is to impart knowledge to all students in your class. You may also assume that all students come to class appreciating knowledge at the level at which you do. This assumption will affect how you approach teaching the knowledge you cherish. Curricula selection, instructional strategies, classroom management, and student-teacher interaction is a short list of items affected by this step on the ladder. The most important thing to remember about this rung on the ladder is that all people make assumptions and that to do so is unavoidable. However, the good news is that assumptions can be critiqued and their accuracy and can be confirmed or dismissed.

Rung 5, Draw Conclusions: You draw conclusions based upon the assumptions you make. You arrive at a decision point. For example, you might decide things about colleagues, students, or parents based upon assumptions you make about the books they read. If the books they read are consistent with the literature you appreciate, you might assume them to be intellectuals and conclude they are as astute as you. On the other hand, if their literature tastes are not consistent with yours, you might conclude them to be not quite as intelligent.

Rung 6, Adopt Beliefs: Beliefs are principles you apply in generalized ways. They govern actions and are the foundations for behavior. They are a powerful aspect of your socialization. At the core of any belief are values and assumptions you have concluded to be true. For example, you may *value* mutual respect. You *assume* that being respectful is an important way to engage in relationships. Therefore, you *conclude* that others are respectful, as well. The belief you hold might be *"Do to others as you would have them do to you."* Beliefs hold tremendous power. They literally determine which data are selected from the vast pool of data surrounding you. As we discuss further later in this chapter, beliefs short-circuit the process and eliminate the steps of considering all data available. How many times have you had an experience, such as not seeing the milk carton in the refrigerator, because it is not in the place you *believed* it should be, only to discover it was in plain view when shown to you by another person? When something like this happens, you are shocked and often embarrassed that you did not see what you were looking for, especially when it was clearly in front of you. However, because your beliefs shape what data you select, it is difficult, if not impossible, to see what you do not believe.

Rung 7, Take Action: You take action based upon what you believe to be true. All outward action arises from subjective processing leading to concrete objected reality. This understanding holds importance because what you are tempted to do is focus on the action or behavior and change it without doing an analysis of the belief generating it. *Real change—sustainable change—occurs beneath the action.*

The Ladder of Inference provides a powerful framework for viewing how actions are born from the beliefs through which you construct reality. Values shape assumptions, which in turn inform conclusions that ultimately formulate beliefs. So how might this work in a real school-based situation? The following example shows how a teacher might move up the Ladder of Inference as he interacts with a student, ultimately taking action based on his own *unexamined* assumptions. Without checking out his assumptions and collecting more data from the student, the action that he takes is harmful to the student because it is based on a distorted picture of reality.

Rung 1: I observe data as a video recorder would view it.

Example: On the first day of class, the teacher enters the room and observes that he has 20 students in his class seated at their desks.

Rung 2: I select data from what I observe.

Example: One of his students, Josh, has his head on the desk. Based on Josh's posture, the teacher observes that the student appears to be asleep.

Rung 3: I apply cultural meaning to the data.

Example: Self-motivation and readiness to learn is of high value to the teacher. Josh appears to be asleep with his head on the desk. According to the teacher's experience, the "good" student is self-motivated.

Rung 4: I make assumptions based on the meaning.

Example: The teacher assumes Josh does not attend to his learning in a very energetic or self-motivating way. He is obviously not intrinsically motivated to learn.

Rung 5: I draw conclusions.

Example: The teacher concludes that Josh is not a "good" student and that he does not *want* to learn because he does not exhibit signs of self-motivation.

Rung 6: I adopt beliefs about the world.

Example: The teacher lives by the principle that "Learning is a matter of self-motivation." He is confident that Josh is not a "good" student and any students associated with him are not serious about school and most likely are not good students either.

Rung 7: I take actions based on my belief.

Example: The teacher works to have Josh and any of his friends or associations removed from his class. He only wants to work with students who will "apply" themselves.

Making assumptions and moving up the Ladder of Inference is a natural process most of us can recognize even though it happens so quickly and automatically that we rarely notice. Given the pervasiveness of cultural biases, however, it is essential that we test our assumptions for accuracy and ask critical questions at each point identified on the ladder. We see the importance of posing critical questions when we view the processes as a closed-circuit reinforcing loop where each step fortifies the next.

Based upon the insights of Gene Bellinger (2004), Figures 3.1 through 3.3 demonstrate how this reinforcing process works. You'll see in Figure 3.1 the seven points building one onto the other. The "R" in the middle of the loop indicates the fortifying nature of the circular processing. In Figure 3.2 you'll see the seven points again. However, the step of processing "observable data" is eliminated. The beliefs short-circuit any new data that might inform action.

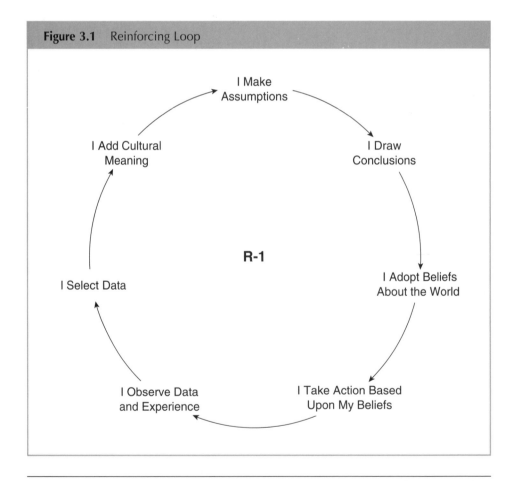

Figure 3.1   Reinforcing Loop

I Make Assumptions

I Add Cultural Meaning

I Draw Conclusions

R-1

I Select Data

I Adopt Beliefs About the World

I Observe Data and Experience

I Take Action Based Upon My Beliefs

SOURCE: Reprinted with permission from Gene Bellinger. *Ladder of Inference: Short Circuiting Reality* (2004). http://www.systems-thinking.org/loi/loi.htm

Figure 3.2 Reinforcing Loop Short-Circuited by Beliefs

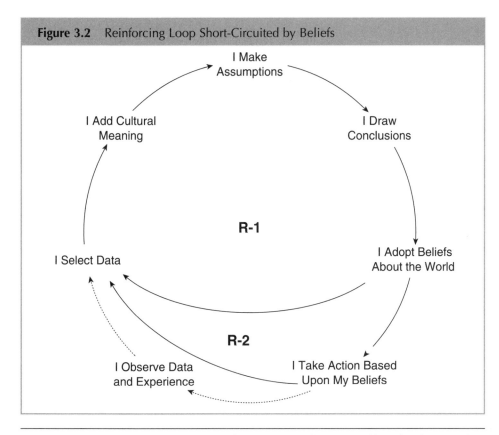

SOURCE: Reprinted with permission from Gene Bellinger. *Ladder of Inference: Short Circuiting Reality* (2004). http://www.systems-thinking.org/loi/loi.htm

Figure 3.3 shows how raising critical questions at each juncture in the reinforcing process opens up the circuit once again so more data informs action. Notice that the questions focus on how "I" might respond to another that might be different than me. Cultural proficiency is about educators being fully aware of their biases and displaying a willingness to examine them in order to better serve students and their families.

Let's review the previous case of the teacher and Josh, applying some of the questions in Figure 3.3. How might the outcome change? Starting at Rung 4, Assumptions, note the difference between "Example" and "Alternate example" resulting from the critical questions asked.

Rung 1: I observe data as a video recorder would view it.

Example: On the first day of class, the teacher enters the room and observes that he has 20 students in his class all seated at their desks. *Critical question:* What is it about my students that I do not notice? Is there more going on than is currently visible to me?

Figure 3.3 Reinforcing Loop with Critical Questions

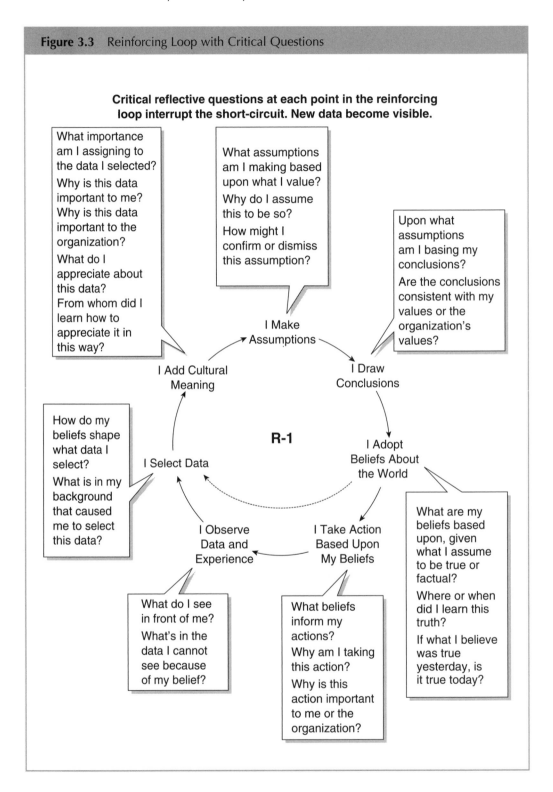

Critical reflective questions at each point in the reinforcing loop interrupt the short-circuit. New data become visible.

What importance am I assigning to the data I selected?

Why is this data important to me?

Why is this data important to the organization?

What do I appreciate about this data?

From whom did I learn how to appreciate it in this way?

What assumptions am I making based upon what I value?

Why do I assume this to be so?

How might I confirm or dismiss this assumption?

Upon what assumptions am I basing my conclusions?

Are the conclusions consistent with my values or the organization's values?

I Make Assumptions

I Add Cultural Meaning

I Draw Conclusions

How do my beliefs shape what data I select?

What is in my background that caused me to select this data?

I Select Data

R-1

I Adopt Beliefs About the World

I Observe Data and Experience

I Take Action Based Upon My Beliefs

What are my beliefs based upon, given what I assume to be true or factual?

Where or when did I learn this truth?

If what I believe was true yesterday, is it true today?

What do I see in front of me?

What's in the data I cannot see because of my belief?

What beliefs inform my actions?

Why am I taking this action?

Why is this action important to me or the organization?

SOURCE: Reprinted with permission from Gene Bellinger. *Ladder of Inference: Short Circuiting Reality* (2004). http://www.systems-thinking.org/loi/loi.htm

Rung 2: I select data from what I observe.

Example: One of the students, Josh, has his head on the desk. Based on Josh's posture, the teacher observes that the student appears to be asleep.

Critical questions: How do I believe students should sit in class? How do my beliefs regarding learning acquisition relate to how students should sit in class?

Rung 3: I apply a culturally understood meaning to the data.

Example: Self-motivation and readiness to learn are of high value to the teacher. Josh's head is on the desk and he appears to be asleep and not engaged.

Critical questions: Why is it important to me that Josh sit with his head up from the desk? What value do I assign to his head being up or down on the desk?

Rung 4: I make assumptions based on the meaning.

Example: The teacher assumes Josh does not attend to his learning in a very energetic or self-motivating way. He is obviously not intrinsically motivated to learn.

Critical questions: How might I confirm or dismiss this assumption? How does this assumption relate to what I value or appreciate?

Alternate Example: The teacher assumes Josh is a highly motivated student but might suffer from the effects of an illness today.

Rung 5: I draw conclusions.

Example: The teacher concludes that the student obviously does not *want* to learn because he does not stay engaged while in the classroom setting.

Critical question: Is this conclusion consistent with my values or the organization's values?

Alternate Example: The teacher concludes that the student is having personal or health issues that keep him from presenting himself in a self-motivating manner.

Rung 6: I adopt beliefs about the world.

Example: The teacher now believes or is *confident* that Josh and any student associated with him are not serious about school and most likely not good students.

Critical question: What are my beliefs based upon, given what I assume to be true or factual?

Alternate example: The teacher believes that any student can have an "off" day and is perfectly capable of being a quality student achieving rigorous coursework.

Rung 7: I take actions based on my belief.

Example: The teacher works to have Josh and any of his friends like him removed from his class.

Critical question: Why is this action important to the organization or me?

Alternate example: The teacher seeks the source of Josh's behavior and finds ways to help him resolve the problem in order to maximize his class performance.

Asking the critical question opens up possibility leading to actions that have a huge impact on the lives of children. As evidenced in the case of Josh, when questioning the assumption at Rung 4, an alternative emerged. By simply asking Josh about his physical state, it is possible to learn that perhaps he works during the evenings to help the family with financial issues, or maybe he is ill on this day. Josh's response to either of these questions could easily change the teacher's conclusion, affecting his belief and ultimately his actions. Equally important, we should examine our values and ultimately our beliefs. As you can see from the previous illustration, not doing so could lead to dire consequences for students.

Reflection

Take a few moments and use the Ladder of Inference template in Table 3.1 to analyze a situation in your professional practice. Think of an interaction with a student, parent, or colleague that left you feeling unfulfilled. Use the template to record your initial observation and then, moving up the rungs on the ladder, continue to probe ever more deeply into your values, assumptions, conclusions, and beliefs. Use the questions in Figure 3.3 to guide your analysis.

Table 3.1   Ladder of Inference Template

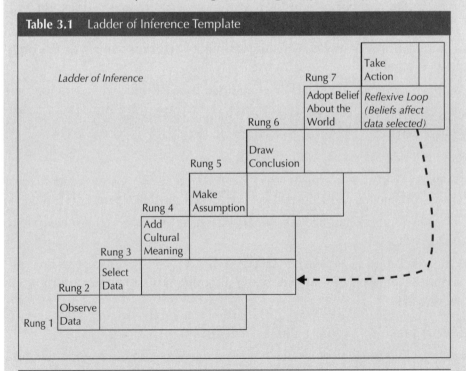

SOURCE: © Franklin CampbellJones, Brenda CampbellJones & Randall B. Lindsey, March 2009.

Cultural Proficiency is an *inside-out* approach to change and requires that you understand effective cross-cultural communication. The Ladder of Inference gives a broad framework for seeing how observable action is a composite of subjective processes. By drilling deeper, it is possible to explore more clearly the dominant values operating in the subjective background. In the next section, you will have the opportunity to uncover these values and discover how they operate in your professional setting. Through a series of processes, you will have the opportunity to identify and make explicit your values. The exercises help you identify the dominant values that guide your actions, and you identify the values that you consider *most* important through a process of elimination using a checklist, responding to reflective questions, and participating in a reflective dialogue process with others.

WHAT I VALUE MOST

When you consider an action by another and something inside says, "That's really not me," most likely you have felt a twinge from a deeply held personal value. *Values* are deeply held views of what we find worthwhile and important. These are associated with that which we appreciate, respect, or cherish. They come from many sources as a part of the socialization process—parents, caregivers, religious teachings, schools, peers, people we admire, and culture. Many are grounded in our childhood experiences while we take on other views as adults.

Table 3.2 presents a list of values commonly associated with our society. While it is a comprehensive list of values, it is by no means an exhaustive source. We encourage you to list additional values that you consider important. Follow the directions in each step to determine your dominant value. It is important to follow each step in sequence, as each step builds upon the next.

Step 1: Values' List

From the list of values in Table 3.2 (both work and personal), select the 10 that are most important to you as components of a valued way of life. If the list does not display a value of yours, we encourage you to add others in the blank spaces provided.

Table 3.2 What I Value Most		
□ Achievement	□ Economic Security	□ Honesty
□ Advancement and Promotion	□ Effectiveness	□ Hope
□ Adventure	□ Efficiency	□ Humor
□ Affection (love and caring)	□ Equal Opportunity	□ Independence
□ Appreciation	□ Equity	□ Influencing Others
□ Arts	□ Ethical Practice	□ Initiative
□ Caring	□ Excellence	□ Inner Harmony
□ Celebration	□ Excitement	□ Integrity
□ Challenges	□ Expertise	□ Intellectual Status
□ Change and Variety	□ Fairness	□ Involvement
□ Close Relationships	□ Fame	□ Job Tranquility
□ Collaboration	□ Fast Living	□ Justice
□ Collegiality	□ Fast-paced work	□ Knowledge
□ Communication (open and honest)	□ Financial gain	□ Leadership
□ Community	□ Flexibility	□ Location
□ Compassion	□ Forgiveness	□ Loyalty
□ Competition	□ Freedom	□ Market Position
□ Confidence	□ Friendships	□ Meaningful Work
□ Cooperation	□ Goals	□ Merit
□ Country	□ Growth	□ Money
□ Creativity	□ Having a Family	□ Nature
□ Decisiveness	□ Helping Other People	□ Nurture
□ Democracy	□ Helping Society	□ Others Not Listed
□ Ecological Awareness	□ High Expectations	□ Perseverance

☐ Personal Development	☐ Responsibility	☐ Traditions
☐ Physical Challenge	☐ Risk Taking	☐ Trust
☐ Pleasure	☐ Security	☐ Truth
☐ Positive Attitude	☐ Self-Respect	☐ Unity
☐ Power and Authority	☐ Self-Sufficiency	☐ Wealth
☐ Pride	☐ Serenity	☐ Wisdom
☐ Privacy	☐ Social Status	☐ Work Under Pressure
☐ Public Service	☐ Sophistication	☐ Work With Others
☐ Purity	☐ Spirituality	☐ Working Alone
☐ Quality	☐ Stability	
☐ Quality Relationships	☐ Status	
☐ Recognition	☐ Supervising Others	
☐ Religion	☐ Support	
☐ Reputation	☐ Time	
☐ Resourcefulness	☐ Togetherness	

SOURCE: Original concept by Robert Niles, vice president of human resources at the Helene Curtis Corporation. Adapted and further developed for educators by the authors.

Step 2: Elimination

A. Now that you have identified 10 values, imagine that you are only permitted to have five values. Decide which five values you would keep. List them here:

1._____   2._____

3._____   4._____

5._____

B. Now imagine that you are only permitted four values. Which would you keep? List them here:

1._____   2._____

3._____   4._____

C. Finally, cross off another, to bring your list down to three values:

1._____   2._____

3._____

Step 3: Reflection

Review your three values in the space provided. Reflect on the following questions using the spaces provided:

Why do I hold these values?

_____

_____

_____

_____

Where did I acquire them? What was the setting or context?

_____

_____

_____

_____

When did I attain them? Describe the timeframe in which these values were attained.

_____

_____

_____

_____

From whom did I attain them? There may be more than one person.

_____

_____

_____

_____

Step 4: Expanding Your Horizon

We can enhance the practice of reflection by reaching beyond our own perspective and coming into the perspective of others. When we do this, our understanding deepens as we explore the worldview of someone else in relationship to our own (Gadamer, 1991). We encourage you to look at the top three values on your list. We invite you to ask two trusted colleagues, friends, or partners to discuss the following questions about your identified values:

a. What do the values mean, exactly? What are you expecting from yourself—even in bad times?

b. How would you behave if these values were prominent and practiced daily at home? At work?

c. In what context might you not practice those values?

Helping Trio

A useful process for reflection with others is called *helping trios*. Helping trios provide a way to scaffold feedback from multiple perspectives giving ample opportunity to increase your understanding. It is a wonderful process for developing shared values and generating common meaning. Invite two trusted colleagues to use the aforementioned process to identify their values. In a group of three, follow the steps as outlined below.

Immediately following this process is a protocol for conducting a dialogue. We suggest you take the time to review it prior to engaging in the helping trio process.

Step 1

Each member of the group identifies as the letter A, B, or C.

Step 2

- A talks about his/her three values while B and C listen without comment (5 minutes).
- B and C ask clarifying questions, i.e. "What did you mean when you said . . . ?" (2 minutes).
- A answers clarifying questions.
- A, B, and C dialogue about A's values (5 minutes) (see dialogue protocol following this section).

Step 3

- B talks about her/his three values while A and C listen.
- A and C ask clarifying questions.
- B answers.
- A, B, and C dialogue about B's three values.

Step 4

- C talks about his/her three values while A and B listen.
- A and B ask clarifying questions.
- C answers.
- A and B dialogue about C's three values.

Step 5

- Freely discuss what you have learned in the process.

DIALOGIC CONVERSATION

Dialogue is a form of conversation oriented towards inquiry for the purpose of developing a collective understanding about a topic. When people dialogue they seek to understand each other's viewpoints and experiences as well as the underlying reasons for these thoughts and actions, while also reflecting on their own viewpoints and experiences. Dialogue bridges the perceived or real differences between speakers. Thus, in dialogue, we gain information and insight not only about others, but also about ourselves.

When dialoguing, it is important to be aware of several crucial points.

- Be aware of your assumptions. Ask, "What assumptions am I making at this moment?" When they become apparent, suspend them so you can be present in the conversation and hear the other person speaking.

- Use probing stems such as "why," "where," "when," and "who." Using these stems allows you to go beneath the surface and look for root causes and connections. Avoid "how" questions at this point, as they lead to strategic conversation, rather than discussions that help with understanding (Habermas, 1990). Consider the following examples:

  o "Why do you think that to be so?"
  o "Where did you learn to think that way?"
  o "When did you find that to be important?"
  o "Who was the person who influenced you in this way?"

- Repeat questions or responses and ask, "Anything else?"
- Ask the other person for examples of what he or she means as they are conveying a story.

This is not an exhaustive list. The intent is to give you ways of drilling deeper into viewpoints while in the dialogue. We suggest several resources for a much deeper treatment to conduct a fruitful dialogue:

- Bohm, David. (1996). *On dialogue.* New York: Routledge.
- Ellinor, Linda, & Gerard, Glenna. (1998). *Dialogue: Rediscovering the transforming power of conversation.* New York: John Wiley & Sons, Inc.
- Lindsey, Randall B., Roberts, Laraine M., & CampbellJones, Franklin. (2005). *The culturally proficient school: An implementation guide for school leaders.* Thousand Oaks, CA: Corwin.

Reflection

In the above activity, you selected a set of values, you winnowed them to a set of core values, and you discussed them with colleagues. What have you learned about yourself in this process?

_____

_____

_____

_____

What have you learned about your colleagues and their values? In what ways are you similar? In what ways are you different? Use the space below to record your responses.

_____

_____

_____

_____

What you value shapes what you come to appreciate. Values like respect, honesty, or integrity act as internal regulators that guide what you assume to be true and ultimately shape your beliefs about how we should behave in relationships with others.

BELIEFS INVENTORY

Beliefs are principles by which we live. They give us confidence that the actions we take are correct and true. It is clear from the discussion of the Ladder of Inference that beliefs are extremely important because all of our conscious actions are predicated upon what we believe. Stated differently, we do not consciously act absent of a belief. A teacher prepares a lesson because she has a belief regarding fundamentals of organization and readiness; the nurse listens to a patient's description of ailments because he believes this is a good source of information for treatment; and, while driving an automobile, we drive in an assigned lane and believe others willfully do the same. These are examples of how beliefs shape action and literally arrange the world in which we live.

In this section, we encourage you to complete a cultural proficiency beliefs inventory. This exercise helps gauge your alignment with the principles of cultural proficiency. The Guiding Principles of Cultural Proficiency are a set of core beliefs that guide the actions of educators in overcoming the Barriers to Cultural Proficiency. Adopting these principles is extremely important for providing equitable academic achievement for each child in our schools. Employing cultural proficiency as a lens to view school policies and practices leads to transformed school processes and structures that ensure a school environment that facilitates for each child. A quick review of the six principles of cultural proficiency (Lindsey, Nuri-Robins, & Terrell, 2003) is as follows:

1. Culture is a predominant force.

   Acknowledge culture as a predominant force in shaping behaviors, values, and institutions. Although you may be inclined to take offense at the behaviors that differ from yours, remind yourself that it may not be personal; it may be cultural.

2. People are served in varying degrees by the dominant culture.

   What works well in organizations and in the community for you, and others who are like you, may work against members of other cultural groups. Failure to make such an acknowledgment puts the burden for change on one group.

3. People have both personal identities and group identities.

   Although it is important to treat all people as individuals, it is also important to acknowledge the group identity of individuals. Actions must be taken with the awareness that the dignity of a person is not guaranteed unless the dignity of his or her people is also preserved.

4. Diversity within cultures is vast and significant.

   Since diversity within cultures is as important as diversity between cultures, it is important to learn about cultural groups not as monoliths such as women, Asians, Latinos, Blacks, Whites, gays, and lesbians, but as the complex and diverse groups that they are. To explain further, within the group we call White, there are huge cultural differences (Catholics, Protestants, Irish Catholics, Irish Protestants, Irish, Jews, Germans, etc.). Often, because of the social status and economic differences in the United States, there will be more in common across cultural lines than within them.

5. Each group has unique cultural needs.

   Each cultural group has unique needs that cannot be met within the boundaries of the dominant culture. Expressions of one group's cultural identity do not imply disrespect for yours. Make room in your organization for several paths that lead to the same goal.

6. The best of both worlds enhances the capacity of all.

   When people adopt practices of other cultures that improve their ability to communicate and problem solve cross-culturally, they are more effective both for themselves and for those with whom they work.

CULTURAL PROFICIENCY BELIEFS INVENTORY

Step 1

This inventory examines the alignment of your beliefs to the Guiding Principles of Cultural Proficiency. Answer the questions intuitively. Marking the number one (1) indicates you agree with the statement. Marking the number zero (0) indicates disagreement or uncertainty with the statement.

1 = I agree

0 = I disagree or I am uncertain

___ 1. I am a member of a cultural group.

___ 2. The dominant culture marginalizes many people in this country.

___ 3. I receive benefits from identifying with my cultural group.

___ 4. Fear of the unknown leads to false assumptions.

___ 5. General practices in public schools reflect the experiences of the dominant culture.

___ 6. Cross-cultural experiences are additive.

___ 7. Culture is ever-present.

___ 8. White privilege exists in America.

___ 9. Guaranteeing the dignity of an individual involves valuing his/her cultural group.

___10. Within my group identity, various cultures exist.

___11. One's perceived social status affects one's behavior and motivation to achieve.

___12. Crossing cultural borders enhances life.

___13. Culture is about my values, assumptions, and beliefs and the actions I take.

___14. I experience privilege when I am part of the dominant group.

___15. Assimilated groups adopt the cultural norms of the dominant group.

__16. More differences can exist between individuals within a cultural group than between cultural groups.

__17. Each cultural group has unique needs that cannot be met within the boundaries of the dominant culture.

__18. Diversity can be equated to strength.

__19. My cultural biases allow me to prejudge behavior that differs from mine.

__20. What benefits some in the workplace may work against others in different cultural groups.

__21. Statements that separate a person from his/her group (e.g., "You're different; you're not like those other ____s.") are offensive.

__22. When considering lifestyles and values, upper-class African Americans share more in common with upper-class European Americans than they do with lower-class African Americans.

__23. When others express their group's cultural identity, they are not implying disrespect for my cultural identity.

__24. Multiple voices at the table enhance quality.

__25. My culture shapes my behaviors, values, and beliefs.

__26. Placing the burden for equitable change only on members of nondominant groups is unjust.

__27. To survive, members of nondominant groups must learn the norms and values of the dominant group.

__28. General knowledge about groups is useful, but authentic cultural knowledge is gained one person at a time.

__29. Leaders should use cultural differences as opportunities to strengthen learning.

__30. Communicating cross-culturally is important.

__31. I am multicultural.

__32. The dominant culture benefits many people in this country.

__33. Identifying as an individual benefits me.

__34. False assumptions can lead to stereotyping.

__35. Members of the dominant group have their needs met through normal activity in the workplace.

__36. Learning about the values of others expands my understanding of people.

__37. I cannot *not* have a culture.

__38. In America, race is a definer for social and economic status.

__39. Reinforcing a negative stereotype about a group is insulting to its members.

__40. Diversity within cultures is as important as diversity among cultures.

__41. The way I am perceived by peers and supervisors influences my behavior.

__42. Communicating my belief to others improves chances of better practices.

__43. Rules (written and unwritten), norms, and climate are reflections of an organization's culture.

__44. Membership in the dominant culture is often invisible to those in the dominant culture.

__45. Assimilation lessens the discomfort of members of the dominant group.

__46. I have more in common with some members from different cultural groups than I do with some members of my own cultural group.

__47. To provide responsible service, I must create multiple paths to the same goal.

__48. Learning how others do things provides the opportunity for me to improve.

__49. "White" is a culture in America.

__50. Marginalization and privilege exist in my school/organization.

__51. My group identity and my individual identity are of equal importance.

__52. People from different racial/ethnic cultural groups may be more alike than different due to being from similar socioeconomic backgrounds.

__53. Inviting the expression of multiple cultures does not mean that I give up my cultural identity.

__54. We are stronger as a society because of our diversity.

__55. I make assumptions based on my cultural and personal values.

__56. I have the responsibility to engage and adapt to cultural differences.

__57. Membership in the dominant group allows for unawareness of the norms and values of different cultural groups.

__58. I hold generalizations about groups that may not be accurate.

__59. Freedom of religion is an expression of unique cultural needs.

__60. I miss opportunities when I fail to draw upon the multiple perspectives around me.

Scoring

Write your number, "0" or "1," for each item in the appropriate cell. Add the cells in each column and total them below.

Guiding Principle 1	Guiding Principle 2	Guiding Principle 3	Guiding Principle 4	Guiding Principle 5	Guiding Principle 6
_____ 1.	_____ 2.	_____ 3.	_____ 4.	_____ 5.	_____ 6.
_____ 7.	_____ 8.	_____ 9.	_____ 10.	_____ 11.	_____ 12.
_____ 13.	_____ 14.	_____ 15.	_____ 16.	_____ 17.	_____ 18
_____ 19.	_____ 20.	_____ 21.	_____ 22.	_____ 23.	_____ 24.
_____ 25.	_____ 26.	_____ 27.	_____ 28.	_____ 29.	_____ 30.
_____ 31.	_____ 32.	_____ 33.	_____ 34.	_____ 35.	_____ 36.
_____ 37.	_____ 38.	_____ 39.	_____ 40.	_____ 41.	_____ 42.
_____ 43.	_____ 44.	_____ 45.	_____ 46.	_____ 47.	_____ 48.
_____ 49.	_____ 50.	_____ 51.	_____ 52.	_____ 53.	_____ 54.
_____ 55.	_____ 56.	_____ 57.	_____ 58.	_____ 59.	_____ 60.
_____ Total	_____ Total	_____ Total	_____ Total	_____ Total	_____ Total
Culture is a predominant force.	People are served in varying degrees by the dominant culture.	Group identity is as important as individual identities.	Diversity within cultures is vast and significant.	Each group has unique cultural needs.	The best of both worlds enhances the capacity of all.

SOURCE: Franklin CampbellJones, Brenda CampbellJones, Randall B. Lindsey, and John Krownapple.

Interpreting Your Score

The total score in each column can range from 0 to 10. On a scale of 0 to 10, each total score indicates how much you agree with that particular principle of cultural proficiency. The closer you are to a total score of 10 for any given category signifies a greater agreement with the principle in that column. For example, a score of 3 in the column "Culture is a predominant force" indicates that you are of lesser agreement with that principle. In contrast, a score of 9 would indicate strong agreement with that principle. More importantly, scores closely aligned with guiding principles suggest a worldview associated with the right side of the Cultural Proficiency Continuum and that you are better equipped to use the Five Essential Elements as standards of cultural competency. A low score (below 6) indicates you would have difficulty overcoming the Barriers to Cultural Proficiency because you hold a worldview that is aligned with the left side of the Cultural Proficiency Continuum.

Reflection

Review your score for each guiding principle. What do your scores indicate about your alignment with the core principles of cultural proficiency?

_____

_____

_____

_____

How might your alignment influence your decisions and behaviors?

_____

_____

_____

_____

What possible challenges exist when your score is 5 or less?

_____

_____

_____

_____

Given a low score with a guiding principle, what will you do to align yourself with the values expressed in that principle?

_____

_____

_____

_____

GOING DEEPER

Understanding that our values, assumptions, and beliefs are always present is central to Cultural Proficiency's *inside-out* process. "To put your beliefs on hold is to cease to exist as ourselves for moment—and that is not easy," states Delpit. "It is painful as well, because it means turning yourself inside out, giving up your own sense of who you are, and being willing to see yourself in the unflattering light of another's angry gaze. It is not easy, but it is the only way to learn what it might feel like to be someone else and the only way to start the dialogue" (1995, pp. 46–47).

It helps to be mindful of what exists in your background that shapes your worldview, because this perspective gives rise to your action. Take a moment and be mindful of how you are feeling at this moment. Is it exciting work for you to explore the bases for your cross-cultural "being-ness"? Is it a bit scary? This important work enhances your effectiveness on the way to working with people culturally different from you.

4 Morality

Motivation, Purpose, and Intent

Although the role of government is important, the enforcement of civil rights transcends federal actions. Enforcement is rather a larger responsibility of American society; its failure lies within the confines of the nation's morals and mores.

—Low and Clift, 1981

Throughout this book, we make the argument that cultural proficiency is an *inside-out* process leading to transformational change for cultural responsiveness and responsibility. This transformational process involves recognizing who you are as a moral being and your commitment to doing what is right and just, even in the face of overwhelming odds and criticism. Using cultural proficiency as an *inside-out* process, you are increasingly aware of your values and the influence they have in shaping assumptions about self and others. You become a student of the decisions you make and how your ensuing actions are founded upon beliefs that you frame as fundamental truths. On the cultural proficiency journey, you are keenly aware that the actions you take, as concrete and objective as they may appear, are based upon a series of subjective processes. Moreover, you realize that others are engaged in the same processes as you are and that what they see as objective action is as tenuous as your own.

In Chapter 3 we state, "Real change—sustainable change—occurs beneath the action." Essentially, what this means is that if you want behaviors to change in classrooms, schools, or school systems, you will have to attend to the driver of the action—the belief.

However, what happens when your actions are inconsistent with your values or your beliefs? How is it that you might come to do something that you do not value or believe? In a recent seminar, a participant proclaimed, "It is not that we don't know what to do to educate children to meet high standards, it is just that we care about our jobs more and don't want to ruffle any feathers." What motivates you to act outside of moral principles?

Sergiovanni (1992) sought answers to questions of this kind in his discussion on moral leadership. He classified actions in three distinct rules. Highlighted in Table 4.1, we list them here with an example illustrating each.

1. *What gets rewarded gets done.* Extrinsic gains are achieved through instrumental devices that motivate people and are a means of calculating involvement of individuals and organizations. People do things as a matter of transaction or exchanges seen as gains that come from outside of themselves, rather than using a principle to guide their action. For example, you review student test data to assess student achievement because of contract stipulations or because No Child Left Behind (NCLB, 2001) holds you accountable for student gains through adequate yearly progress reports. If not mandated in the contract or legislation, you would not perform the task of reviewing data. Our workshop participant found herself adhering to this rule in her proclamation caring for her "job more." In this case, she elected to act according to the external force—a paycheck—that *made* her perform the action of educating children in a way that she did not necessarily believe was proper.

2. *What is rewarding gets done.* Intrinsic gains are a matter of internal expression. People move into action because what they choose to do is fundamental to who they are. There is personal and professional benefit for taking this action. For example, you review student test data to hone your skills at teaching math, reading, art, and so on. It is painfully obvious that our workshop participant possessed knowledge and skills to teach her students, but failed to engage in educating her students for the sake of the external motivation—*not ruffling feathers and keeping her job.* She has chosen to forsake intrinsic expression for the purpose of externally motivated gains.

3. *What is good gets done.* Motivation is a matter of duty. One moves into action by principles that dictate a sense of responsibility for the right action. For example, you review test data because of an obligation to be responsive to the academic achievement of each student and the benefit to the larger society. What might happen if our participant was motivated in this way? Would her principles regarding the education of children override the external motivation of not ruffling feathers and keeping her job?

Table 4.1	Three Rules of Motivation		
Rules	*Why People Behave*	*Motivational Types*	*Involvement*
1. *What gets rewarded gets done.*	Extrinsic gains	Instrumental	Calculated
2. *What is rewarding gets done.*	Intrinsic gains	Expressive	Intrinsic
3. *What is good gets done.*	Duty/obligation	Moral	Moral

SOURCE: Thomas Sergiovanni (1992).

A criterion for success on the cultural proficiency journey is self-education motivated by a deep intrinsic awareness of the need for a moral response to others that occurs in a constructive manner. Cultural proficiency assumes an orientation of esteeming the culture of another. As a culturally proficient individual and organization, the focus is on what emanates from within and how it manifests outwardly to engage with others. It is a moral focus toward ethical duty, where one is responsive to and responsible for someone else.

Reflection

After studying Table 4.1, think about what motivates you to educate others. Are you largely involved because of extrinsic gains, intrinsic gains, or obligation and duty?

_____

_____

_____

_____

MORAL PURPOSE

In Chapter 3, we established that aware or not, you maintain values and beliefs as well as make assumptions about others. Whether a teacher, counselor, or principal, this is a natural process. It is important to know that you express personal aspects of your morality. However, it is equally important to understand that the school conveys aspects of morality in the collective. Members of the school community coalesce to express dominant values, assumptions, and beliefs. These congregated values, assumptions, and beliefs eventually crystallize throughout the organization in the form of policies, procedures, and practices, as well as in the very architecture of facilities that house the school community. Given that these elements may comprise the morality of the school, this leads to an extremely compelling question: *What is the moral purpose of schooling?* What might schooling look like if we were to view it through a moral purpose? What if we view moral purpose as our desired intent based upon what we value, assume, and believe to be right, wrong, fair, or just?

Fullan (2003) argues rather convincingly that moral purpose should be front and center of all professional actions in the educational setting. "Let me be explicit," he states. "The only goal worth talking about is transforming the current school system so that large-scale, sustainable, continuous reform becomes built in" (p. 29). For Fullan, "built-in" is about becoming better at providing equitable education for each child and the effort of being better is at the center of the work of a school rather than an add-on after-school program established at the fringe of instruction and curricula processes. Fullan goes on to say, "Moral purpose of the highest order is having a system where all students learn, the gap between high and low performance becomes greatly reduced, and what people learn enables them to be successful citizens and workers in a morally based knowledge society" (p. 29).

Fullan's passionate argument provides criteria worthy of consideration relative to the tenets of cultural proficiency:

- All students and teachers benefit in terms of identified desirable goals.
- The gap between high and low performers becomes less as the bar for all is raised.
- Ever-deeper educational goals are pursued.
- The culture of the school becomes so transformed that continuous improvement relative to the previous three components becomes built in. (p. 31)

From Fullan's perspective, knowledge and technologies used in education are in service of moral purpose. Stated through the lens of cultural proficiency, *the technical is always in service of the ethical.* Literally, all of the techniques and processes—testing, policies, procedures, learning communities, etc.—used in schools are in service of moral purpose, that is, what we *intend* for schooling.

As you think about moral purpose, what is your reaction to Fullan's criteria and his statement of the "goal" for school systems? How does his goal fit with what you consider to be the goal of schools? How do you think your colleagues view the purpose of schooling?

_____

_____

_____

_____

INTENT: OUGHT AND WILL

As you can see from Fullan's argument in the previous section, moral purpose is an important feature for setting the course of action in schools. Getting in touch with the essence of purpose essentially guides your actions. However, knowing the purpose and reconciling the tension of doing the required action sometimes is the center of difficulty for bringing about change. As in the case of the workshop participant earlier who clearly understood the purpose of "educating children to high standards," she was not able to bring herself to do (for whatever reasons) the required steps to make this happen for children. What was required of her was a shift in worldview, from what is expressed on the left side of the Cultural Proficiency Continuum to what is expressed on the right. Her inability or unwillingness to reconcile the tension between what she _ought_ to do and what she was _willing_ to do put her in a position of fostering a climate in her classroom that is culturally destructive, incapacitating, and blind for her students.

How things "ought" to be springs from an expression of your values and beliefs about a given situation. Our teacher above clearly understood what she ought to do according to the importance she placed upon teaching children—educate each child to high academic standards. However, her unwillingness to move forward thwarted the expression of what she valued. She is the perfect illustration of the place where educators frequently find themselves—caught between what they _ought_ (principle) to do and what they _will_ (movement to desired action) do (Habermas, 1990).

This conundrum captures powerful words spoken by Asa Hilliard (1991) when he proclaimed what he believed to be the central problem in the educational system's inability to educate all children to high standards. Hilliard made a declaration and posed a powerful question, "We have one and only one problem: Do we truly wish to see each and every child in this nation develop to the peak of his or her capacities?" (p. 36). Perhaps more potent than the actual statement was the title of Hilliard's article, "Do We Have the Will to Teach All Children?" His question reaches beyond the technical aspects of education directly into the ethical, questioning whether teachers, counselors, and administrators want all children to receive a rigorous education or are only intent on educating a select few.

What is the essence of your "oughtness" and how does it coincide with your willingness to make it happen? It is the position of this book that educators must have the will to respond in a culturally competent way when providing rigorous academic education for children. This requires that you ethically embrace the child's culture—traditions, values, and beliefs—and follow through accordingly.

As you read in Chapter 2, the Principles of Cultural Proficiency (repeated in Table 4.2 for your convenience) undergird the actions you take as a culturally competent educator. For most, it takes effort to reconcile what we ought to do with what we are willing to do, particularly if the values and beliefs you embrace are new. Perhaps the Principles of Cultural Proficiency offer a new worldview or, at a minimum, they express your values in ways very different from how you have previously expressed them. In either case, the struggle to reconcile can be difficult and will require a great deal of conscious effort on your part.

Table 4.2 Cultural Proficiency Principles
1. Culture is a predominant force in people's lives.
2. The dominant culture serves people in varying degrees.
3. People have both personal identities and group identities.
4. Diversity within cultures is vast and significant.
5. Each individual and each group has unique cultural value.

A compelling case illustrating this struggle occurs in a study of heterosexual White males who make it their mission in life to ensure racial justice in American society. Conducted by Brenda CampbellJones (2002), the study sought to address causes for the actions of these men as they pursued this goal. CampbellJones, an African American female, states that she was drawn to the research in pursuit of what to her was a transfixing question. She wanted to know what shaped the actions of those who have historically benefited in a highly racialized society to work at dismantling a system that gave them the benefit of privilege. Her piercing insight as to what she means by "privileged" gives us a clue as to what motivated her to conduct the study.

> One is compelled to recognize that oppressed groups seeking equality needed to be amended into the Constitution in their quest for justice. On the other hand, heterosexual White men as a group, the unstated norm, have never needed to be amended into the Constitution. (p. 4)

What motivated these men to place their benefits, and in some cases their lives, in jeopardy? Why would they personally commit to social justice values and subsequently, with conscious intent, take action accordingly? This becomes more intriguing when you consider "whether consciously or unconsciously, they have enjoyed power, as manifested in the form of privilege or entitlement, as part of our history and economic status in this country" (p. 4).

CampbellJones located key elements that suggest reasons for the men in the study's motivation.

1. Each man had a relationship with a significant person early in life where the principle of "the golden rule" was central to their teaching. This principle became the moral anchor for all intentional actions for eradicating racism.

2. Each man experienced a racial dilemma triggering a critical emotional event that tested their commitment to this principle. Their ability to act congruently with the principle triggered a snowballing effect reinforcing further consistent behaviors.

3. Each man consciously took intentional action to eradicate racial injustice although they were immersed in an environment of privilege and entitlement leading them to experience competing values that suggested they enjoy these benefits. They consciously dismissed privileged situations and sought to elevate those historically disenfranchised in society.

4. Each man had a relationship with someone often at the receiving end of social injustice, in all cases African-American. They clearly understood their unique position of possible blindness to privilege because they benefited from privileged perspectives, acts, policies, and structures in society. They trusted and relied upon the perspectives and the experiences of others not receiving benefits to be their cross-cultural informant—to help them see what they could not see.

5. Each man engaged in a process of critical reflective analysis. They constantly participated in critical self-critique relative to their principle—the golden rule—and their action.

Figure 4.1 depicts the model CampbellJones created illustrating the above elements as a fluid, overlapping dynamic. The concentric circles encapsulating the elements intersect with the principles—the point of moral foundation for ethical reasoning and judgment. Intentional action surrounds the moral foundation located at the center of the diagram.

Figure 4.1   Theoretical Model of Intentional Moral Action for Racial Justice

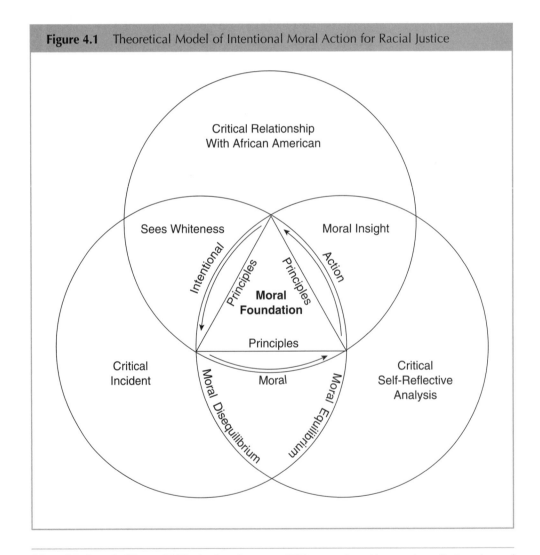

SOURCE: CampbellJones (2002). *Against the stream: White men who act in ways to eradicate racism and white privilege/entitlement in the United States of America.* Claremont Graduate School.

CampbellJones observed that when the men in her study encountered a critically disturbing situation regarding racial injustice they were ethically thrown off balance. They experienced an inward disequilibrium as they struggled to make a decision about the right action to take in their circumstance. This is an important observation. Most ethical decisions are subconscious and are located in the background of our experience in a place Habermas (1990) terms "lifeworld."

The lifeworld is the operating backdrop that one draws upon when engaged in the process of understanding others. It is the sum total of life experiences, providing the context from which you form presuppositions, as you go about interpreting things around you. Whatever the problem or situation, you draw upon the lifeworld to make sense of it. A good way to view the lifeworld is to imagine yourself surrounded by a horizon establishing the parameters of your vision. Within these parameters are patterns, rules, and regulations that shape your worldview. A dominant feature of the lifeworld is that it provides the context from which all interpretations occur. "It is all pervasive, existing as background which disappears before we can really identify it," states Brookfield (2005, p. 10). "It," he continues, "saturates our conversations with cultural knowledge of which we are always already familiar." For the men in CampbellJones' study, their lifeworld experience included a saturation of privilege and entitlement that was in competition with their belief of "the golden rule." As a result, they found it necessary to raise their decision-making processes in cases involving racial issues to a conscious level where they could intentionally focus upon this moral principle learned early in life. In other words, they forcibly connected what they *"ought"* to do (action grounded in principle) with what they were *"willing"* to do (action grounded in intent).

CampbellJones' findings help us visualize the nature of the inner struggle to do the "right" thing when faced with circumstances involving equity and social justice. Study the following case from CampbellJones' research to gain a clearer view of this struggle in action.

Michael (pseudonym) is the grandson of an active Ku Klux Klansman. A 35-year-old activist, he has worked to eradicate racism and oppression since he was 15 years old. He lives with his wife and children in the South and travels throughout the country speaking and challenging issues of privilege and racism. He is straightforward in his approach and believes that racism is an issue that needs to be addressed head-on or very little will change for the oppressed.

Although Michael's mother was raised by a Klansman, she did not want her son to grow up as an oppressor of the less fortunate, as her own mother had raised her. She was deliberate in her actions and was careful to teach him values that were different from those of her own upbringing. Furthermore, she made sure that he was socialized in an environment with Black people—those around him who were historically oppressed. She wanted to be sure that Michael learned that discrimination was wrong. This, according to him, was providential.

> I was very fortunate to have been able to see those connections based largely on the way that I was raised. I was blessed really to have parents, particularly my mother, who were very clear, although not overly political and certainly not activists, but very aware of the need to socialize me in a way that would present the greatest likelihood of turning me into someone who was committed to antioppression or committed to liberation. (CampbellJones, 2002, p. 87)

Because of Michael's socialization—the values and beliefs that were intentionally made explicit to him by his mother—he noticed very early in his life the privileges afforded him because he was White. Unlike his Black friends, he received preferential treatment by other White people. This disparity in treatment was unsettling.

> When you have the cornerstone foundation that I had going into elementary school and seeing that your Black friends were treated quite inferior and seeing yourself treated better at five, six and seven years old, you clearly don't know what to make of that. You know it bothers you and can't quite put your finger on it. (p. 88)

The shaping of Michael's morality was reinforced by his mother, who modeled for him "right and wrong" when it came to issues of equity. He recounted a situation when she stood up to her own mother for wanting to teach him racist behaviors. Michael's grandmother challenged his mom about the way she was raising him to associate with Blacks. His mother was quite clear in her response. "He's not your child and I am not going to let my child grow up to think the things that you tried to make me think," Michael recalled her stating.

His mother didn't stop there. Her quest for equity was demonstrated not only within her family, but in her daily work as well. Although not considered an activist, she responded with a helping hand to others as they suffered daily from systematic oppression. Her examples helped shape Michael's morality. He recalled a major incident in school with a teacher where his mother refused to succumb to conventional behavior, but instead acted on behalf of the greater good. Michael recalls:

I remember there was a period of time where I was so identified with Black people, not only in my own mind but also clearly in the minds of teachers and other students at the school, that I was reaping the negative consequences of that. Despite the fact I was being placed into the advanced track, I had teachers who gave me a really difficult time. I was perceived as a troublemaker because of my affiliation with Black students.

I didn't get in a lot of trouble, but you could just see it. It was very clear to me. One of my teachers actually made a comment to my mother, at one point. She really did not like me and particularly had a hard time with how close I was to the Black kids in the school. She told my mother that "any White parent that would let their child hang around with savages [was] not fit to be a parent." This had to affect her teaching, not only of me but also obviously of any other child. And my mother, to her credit, had this woman fired within a week. (p. 120)

Michael is open about his own assumptions about race. He believes that "members of the dominant group tend to think, of course, that the dominant [White] perspective is the norm. Whites see it as the 'normal' view point" (p. 129). Being a member of the dominant White group, Michael is candid about the difficulty he has in reconciling his morality with the privileges afforded to him by a racialized society that is clearly in conflict with his early moral principles of equity and equality.

I too, have been shaped, molded, and affected by racism. Throughout my life, even if it's just momentarily, I have bought into the negative stereotypes or the images [of historically oppressed people]. I had a hard time resisting these images, or at the very least found myself putting forth weak efforts against them because the conditioning is so strong. (p. 120)

Being committed to resist oppression is fruitless without dismantling its counterpart. Michael stressed with certainty:

It [White privilege] is about the fact that I'm being preferentially treated, that I'm being favored and that their oppression is the flip side of that. Intimately connected to that is my preference and my preference is intimately related to their oppression and not two sides of different coins, but two sides of one coin. (p. 110)

It is clear that Michael struggles daily to reconcile his beliefs with his actions in his work to eradicate racial injustice. He does this primarily because of the ever-present benefits he has received resulting from his societal racial classification as a White male. He strains to maintain balance by intentionally reconciling his actions with his principles. "This effort to maintain a balance," states CampbellJones, "allows for cognitive development and effective thought processes" (p. 162).

Michael's journey highlights the incessant struggle that occurs when attempting emancipation from the lifeworld experience. What complicates the emancipation effort is that a person must use the very patterns within the lifeworld experience to inform the attempt to break free. In other words, Michael has to work against old background patterns, while using the old background patterns in the process of establishing new patterns. As Michael said earlier regarding his battle against the temptations of accepting the benefits of privilege received as a White male raised in a racialized society, "I had a hard time resisting them or, at the very least, found myself putting forth weak efforts against them because the conditioning is so strong." By conditioning, he means understandable patterns of doing things in the old way. The old way is the familiar way, or lifeworld experience operating as background.

In many ways, Michael's struggle is emblematic of most, if not all, educators. Although his story is about the effects of racism and the conundrum of white privilege, there are many forms of systematic oppression—sexism, homophobia, ableism, religious discrimination—that are present in schools on a daily basis. The critical questions for educators are: *Who benefits and who is at the margins based upon the dominant culture maintained by all members of the organization?* What are the patterns, rules, and regulations that govern you as you interpret your relationships with the children in your classroom? What patterns are operational in your background and determine how you come to understand parents and the communities in which they live? If your lifeworld experience is about educating *some* children to achieve well academically, how do you change these patterns given that they shape the way you approach the very issue of educating *every child* to achieve?

MASTERING THE DILEMMA

For most educators, these thorny questions present a dilemma. As in the cases of Michael and our workshop participant, the events they faced put them in a situation where they had to make hard choices. A dilemma is a situation where you must make a choice between two conflicting right answers and either choice leads you in opposing directions. A dilemma comprises the following characteristics:

1. You must make a decision between two opposing options.

2. Either choice you make is "right" because your values support your action.

Whatever the eventual action, you feel ensnared because your values and beliefs are both right. Because they are both right choices, they lead you to a feeling of self-condemnation. Consider the classic case of Heinz to gain further insight of a dilemma.

> In Europe, a woman was near death from a special kind of cancer. There was one drug that the doctors thought might save her. It was a form of radium that a druggist in the same town had recently discovered. The drug was expensive to make, but the druggist was charging ten times what the drug cost him to make. He paid $200 for the radium and charged $2,000 for a small dose of the drug. The sick woman's husband, Heinz, went to everyone he knew to borrow the money, but he could only get together about $1,000, which is half of what it cost. He told the druggist that his wife was dying and asked him to sell it cheaper or let him pay later. But the druggist said, "No, I discovered the drug and I'm going to make money from it." So Heinz got desperate and broke into the man's store to steal the drug for his wife. Should the husband have done that? (Kohlberg, 1973, p. 638)

What are Heinz's choices? He could choose to beg for more money, hoping to get it in time before his wife dies from her ailment. However, the probability of not finding the funds is high. Besides, Heinz values rugged individualism and that each man stands on his own. On the other hand, he could steal the medication and violate a deeply held value of having respect for what rightfully belongs to others. Yet, stealing the medication would save his wife from certain death. What would you do in Heinz's situation? The greater point from Heinz's circumstance underscores the elements of a dilemma. Either choice made is an entrapment where he experiences self-condemnation because his values dictate two conflicting right responses.

Educators are plagued with dilemmas on a daily basis where they face conflicting "right" choices resulting in competing "right" actions. It might be the act of educating each child to achieve rigorous academic standards in light of an appreciation you have for certain learning styles expressed by some children associated with learning the content. Yet, your dilemma may spring from a value you have of cherishing a strong positive relationship with coworkers and the need to have positive conversations about children. The dilemma might be that most conversations you have with coworkers about students are not overly positive. Review the following case. Although a fictional composite of real events, consider how you would respond.

> Amy entered the teacher's lounge after an invigorating morning with her students and eagerly retrieved her lunch from the refrigerator. While standing with the refrigerator door open, she overheard a conversation by colleagues where they discussed their students using language associated with the left side of the Cultural Proficiency Continuum (Chapter 2). Their comments were destructive and incapacitating caricatures of the children in their classes. One teacher referred to a group of children as either "plums, prunes, or pits." The table broke into spontaneous laughter from her comment. "And we know who the pits are," another quipped. The attitude of viewing children as negatives really distressed Amy. Raised in a family of educators, she expected more of teachers. She slowly closed the refrigerator door and turned toward her colleagues.

What should Amy do? What are her options? Perhaps she approaches her colleagues and expresses her disappointment in the way they describe the children in the school? However, if she confronts them, will she risk the possibility of alienation? On the other hand, she could ignore a deeply held value of viewing children as positives, take a seat at the table, and join the culturally destructive conversation about students. In which case, she would preserve a deeply held value of maintaining a relationship with fellow teachers. Yet another option might be to leave the teacher's lounge altogether and quietly retreat to her room to have lunch by herself, in which case she accomplishes self-imposed isolation. What should Amy do? What would you do?

_____

_____

_____

_____

The culturally competent educator remains committed to doing what is right and just, in spite of confronting odds and potential criticism that could be overwhelming. Seeing the situation you face as a dilemma unleashes tremendous energy, giving you strength to move through the situation in search of the best possible choice. In Amy's case, identifying her conflicting values helps her see that she is making a clear choice between multiple rights rather that what is right or wrong. She must make the *best* "right" choice. It is "right" that she values a relationship with her colleagues. But, is it the best "right" to choose? It might be an equally good "right" to become secluded in her room. Yet, the best "right" might be to hold firm on her value of educating each child to high academic levels, take a seat with her colleagues, interrupt the negative conversation, and advocate for a rigorous education for all children in the school.

Reflection

Think of a time when your values were challenged and you felt a sense of imbalance. How did you attempt to regain balance?

_____

_____

_____

_____

What are daily indignities that you have witnessed in your work? How did you intercede? What principles guided your actions? If you did not intercede, what principles did you violate? How did you feel by not interceding?

_____

_____

_____

_____

Part II

Case Studies

From Reflection to Action

In the following chapters, you will build on the Guiding Principles by using the Continuum and the Essential Elements to analyze educational cases. There are six cases framed around the three barriers to cultural proficiency. We focus on one barrier per case for the purpose of analysis. However, you will find elements of the three barriers in each case. Listed below is each barrier with the associated cases.

Systems of Oppression: A Superintendent's Predicament and Family First

Resistance to Change: Science Lesson and Public Announcement

A Sense of Privilege and Entitlement: Heart Condition and Early America

While fictional, the cases are composites of real situations in school settings. They contain dilemmas constructed around the barriers to cultural proficiency. When reading the cases, you are encouraged to reflect upon them, hold constructive conversation with colleagues, and consider what you would view as appropriate resolutions as they relate to your values, assumptions, and beliefs. The resources referenced throughout this book are at your disposal: Ladder of Inference, the rules of motivation, and CampbellJones' model of intentional moral action are all intended to deepen your conversations for healthy perspective relative to the Cultural Proficiency Continuum.

We place questions at the end of each case to assist with analysis, reflection, and productive conversation. We consider these as conversation starters and are fully aware that you will pursue challenges far beyond our offerings. It has been our experience there exist real opportunities for your school to transform based upon the quality of conversation you have with colleagues in your workplace. Powerful change happens when teachers, parents, administrators, counselors, custodians, secretaries, and all members of the school staff engage in conversational fellowship. It is in the languaging process (Maturana & Varela, 1992) that real sharing of lifeworlds (Habermas, 1990) happens, where consensus develops, leading to *healthy perspectives*, as identified on the Cultural Proficiency Continuum. You will find that these exercises provide constructive avenues that build your capacity and that of your colleagues' for future actions.

There is no particular order for reading the cases. You are encouraged to read them according to your interest or organizational need. They are perfect for staff meetings to start dialogue using the helping trio process highlighted in Chapter 3 or as a jigsaw process with members of a school team or staff.

5 Barrier 1

Systems of Oppression

O ne barrier to overcome when moving toward cultural proficiency is various systems of oppression. We need to recognize and dismantle historical forms of oppression that are operational in schools. Schools can, by tradition, institutionalize sexism, racism, ethnocentrism, ableism, and homophobia, to list a few, through organizational policies and practices. The persistence of the well-documented academic educational achievement gap (Delpit, 1995; Fullan, 2003; Perie, Moran, & Lutkus, 2005) gives evidence of the lingering affects of these systems as woven into the fabric of schools.

In Chapter 1, we presented the questions below as Barbara Campbell prepared to audit the Oakland Hills School District. Read them again as you prepare to analyze the two cases that follow: *A Superintendent's Predicament* and *Family First.*

- What practices are in the schools that reinforce this barrier? Does the school forcibly track certain students into nonacademic courses? Are new, inexperienced teachers, with the lowest skill levels, assigned to teach students with the greatest needs?
- What policies are in place at the school, or system level, that encourage or support this barrier?
- What artifacts exist that indicate this barrier is in place, e.g., student achievement gaps between demographic groups, inequitable proportionality of student demographic groups in college preparatory courses, etc.?
- What beliefs are present that maintain and propagate these systems, e.g., "I believe that children have innate learning abilities that will allow them to experience certain levels of learning. Some have it and some don't."

CASE 1: A SUPERINTENDENT'S PREDICAMENT

Eduardo Soriano has been superintendent of the Oakland Hills School District for one year. His short tenure at the helm has been quite a challenge. The school system has historically been a successful example in the state, noted for providing high academic education for students. Recently, two schools were identified under new state and federal guidelines as "under performing," a status unfamiliar to the Oakland Hills District.

However, this circumstance now faced by the school system was not a complete surprise to Eduardo. When he was principal, he was fully aware that there were high-achieving schools and low-achieving schools in the Oakland Hills School District. In truth, he felt fortunate to have been a principal in a Westside school that had been, and continues to be, academically successful. He was intently involved in his predecessor's initiatives to confront the encroaching educational inadequacies of the district. As superintendent, he now had to develop plans that were equitable in a fashion that addressed the chronic underachievement of Eastside schools. He embraced the values of cultural proficiency. However, it was becoming increasingly apparent that many in the system did not embrace these values. The view from the top position, as superintendent, was not as he had envisioned it to be while coming up the ranks.

In his meeting with Barbara, he gave candid responses as to the mounting pressures of the job. "It used to be that 'low-performing schools' were known entities but were rarely discussed," Ed stated to Barbara with a sigh. "But let's face it, we have failed to address these 'known issues' for two generations." He shared with Barbara a list of realities with which he had to come to grips:

- Eastside schools had been regarded as training grounds for teachers and administrators who, after demonstrating effectiveness in Eastside schools, were promoted to Westside schools.
- The imbalance of resources to Eastside schools, mostly in terms of human resources, translated into schools with higher turnover rates of educators than Westside schools.
- To try to balance the resources in an equitable fashion that would systemically address the achievement gap would be perceived as taking resources away from Westside schools.
- Failure to effectively address the historical achievement gaps between the two sides of Oakland Hills would risk one or more schools facing state or federal sanctions as "needing improvement."
- Failure to effectively address the historical achievement gaps between African American and English learner students across Oakland Hills, also, would risk one or more schools facing state or federal sanctions as "needing improvement."
- His participation in the Cultural Proficiency Professional Learning Seminars had raised his consciousness about the barriers to culturally proficient practices and he was keenly aware of how he had benefited in his professional advancement from issues of privilege.

There was also pressure mounting over shrinking resources. The budget faced a 3% reduction. Although lay-offs were not forthcoming, fewer funds would affect bus routes and students needed transportation to schools where resources were readily available. In fact, Westside schools, against some opposition, opened their doors to populations of students overflowing from the Eastside community. Many of the Eastside students came from low-cost housing established through the efforts of members of the City Council. In addition, Ed received an e-mail from a highly respected veteran teacher, Tom Pratt, suggesting that some students did not belong at one of the local high schools. Mr. Pratt lobbied for resources for making sure students' "readiness" was up to par for high school entrance into the prestigious Pine Hills High School. Pratt's e-mail came on the heels of a recent newspaper article questioning the quality of students entering the schools with the new influx of residents. The e-mail, through informal channels, managed to make the rounds with members of the governing school board.

Barbara: You seemed anxious when we spoke on the phone. Am I reading this correctly?

Eduardo: Yes, I am a little anxious. We have some things brewing that took me a bit off guard. I expected more people in the schools to be supportive of students. What I am learning is that not everyone is as supportive as I had hoped.

Barbara: What do you mean?

Eduardo: I truly felt people entered the business of education with a sincere desire to love and care for children. My vision is that they wake up everyday and see it as their duty to help kids learn. I know we have it written down in our Mission Statement, but I don't think it is in their hearts.

Barbara: What is your sense of the support for cultural proficiency at the school board level?

Eduardo: I think they are supportive. They have all attended the initial professional development sessions and they frequently discuss how much they have learned. In fact, they talk about how it has affected their personal lives.

Barbara: How have your school district's policies changed as a result of what they have learned?

Eduardo fell backward into his chair. He knew the point of Barbara's question. Attending a fulfilling seminar was a good start. However, the true test of professional learning is whether anything changes enough to result in positive effects on the lives of the children. Although the question posed was about the board, it was equally a question about Eduardo. Unsure of how to respond, Barbara pressed further.

Barbara: Sometimes it takes a little pushing from the superintendent's chair to get people to do what is in their hearts to do. You may have to ask them tough questions and give them the language on which to hang their hats.

Barbara's proposition echoed in Eduardo's mind. Will what is good get done? Did he have the courage to take action for "what is right" and risk a possible backlash? Was there a way he could explain the school system's moral responsibility to better serve communities historically underserved in Oakland Hills in a way that the school board would be able to listen and hear?

Following his meeting with Barbara, Eduardo immediately scheduled a meeting with two members of the school board. Ruth Steinz served as the board chair. She was a lifetime resident of the Oakland Hills Community and had been educated in the Oakland Hills School District. John Ridge moved to the community eight years before and has played an active role in civic affairs.

Eduardo: I am glad you were able to come to the meeting today. I know you are extremely busy. I have something very important to review with you. As you are aware, we have students from communities that have not performed well in meeting Annual Yearly Progress for state academic standards.

Ruth: Seems to me it has been this way all along. As a child, I remember talking about kids from the Eastside community not really doing well in school.

John: Truthfully, Ed, when we moved here, our realtor advised us about the best neighborhoods based upon where the "good" students were located.

Eduardo: Well, that is just it. Every neighborhood should be where the "good" students live. All of the children in our community should be doing well in school.

John: Let's face it; the achievement data does not support that notion. Some kids just do better than others when it comes to academics. On the other hand, you can't find a better sports program than at Eastside High School.

Ruth: Well, Tom, maybe it isn't just about the kids. Maybe it has something to do with the way we do things around here. I have lived here all my life and have a good idea of how things are done.

Eduardo: Well, that is just my concern. We do an outstanding job providing the best teachers, resources, and facilities for most of our students and communities. However, it is becoming increasingly apparent to me that we are shortchanging some of our students.

Honestly, students from Eastside have not done well in school for years and we have known it for years. Maybe there is more to this than just kids.

John: Whoa! That is a pretty serious charge. Are you saying that the school system deliberately holds services from students? It is hard for me to imagine this to be the case. It is going to take a lot to convince me to believe this one.

Eduardo: Well, I have been studying the numbers, and several things jump out at me. Our most experienced and highly educated teachers are concentrated in the Westside schools. The majority of the school district's facility renovation projects happen in Westside schools. Most of the college academic recruitment fairs and tours originate in Westside schools. There are many other things to cite, but these come to mind.

Ruth: Let's suppose we agree with you. What do you propose?

Eduardo: Well, a good place to start is with our district policy. I have scheduled similar meetings with the rest of the board members to get their opinions on this topic. I think we should move this discussion forward, as an agenda item.

Reflection

Questions for Reflection/Discussion

1. What systems of oppression are evident in this case?

_____

_____

_____

_____

2. How has Eduardo benefited from disparate distribution of resources in the Oakland Hills School District?

_____

_____

_____

_____

3. Systems of oppression are artifacts of beliefs held by people who work in the school system. Describe the beliefs of:

Ruth Steinz:

_____

_____

_____

_____

John Ridge:

_____

_____

_____

_____

Eduardo Soriano:

_____

_____

_____

_____

4. Toward the end of the dialogue, Eduardo and Ruth express an emerging worldview that is different from that of John Ridge. How would you characterize these worldviews relative to the cultural proficiency as discussed in Chapter 2?

_____

_____

_____

_____

5. What would you do if you were in Eduardo's situation? How do the values and beliefs you identified in Chapter 3 support the action you propose?

_____

_____

_____

_____

6. Identify two or three oppressive systems in your own school district.

_____

_____

_____

_____

6a. What are the values and beliefs that perpetuate those systems of oppression?

_____

_____

_____

_____

6b. How do *you* benefit, or not benefit, from those systems?

_____

_____

_____

_____

CASE 2: FAMILY FIRST

Blue Lakes Elementary School is another school in the Oakland Hills School District. It has undergone major changes in the past five years. The student population has more than doubled with no signs of stopping. Not only did the school need more buildings, materials, and additional staff to accommodate the overwhelming growth, but they found they did not have the skills to respond to the newly found diversity amongst the staff and the students.

Because of the staggering new student population growth, a variety of cultures emerged that were different from that of the staff and students previously enrolled in the school. The staff's goal had always been to "embrace each other and do whatever it takes" to create a safe and nurturing environment for every one at Blue Lakes Elementary. Everyone on the staff saw his or herself as part of a family and worked diligently to embrace the students as their own. Working with their active Parent Teachers Association, they adopted the slogan "We Are Family." They envisioned all members—students, parents, educators, and community—as family.

From the start, the principal suggested they embark on a journey toward cultural proficiency to help them respond to the growing population of new staff and students. Most of the staff agreed and thought the approach would enhance their skills and strengthen their relationships. Only a few thought the journey was a waste of time. "We are all Americans. I don't know why this cultural proficiency stuff is necessary in the first place," was a typical response from the dissenters. However, the staff moved ahead and embraced the tenets of cultural proficiency, eventually winning over the initial naysayers and gaining full involvement from everyone.

Mrs. Janice McRay sat in her room long after the school day had ended. She thought about the most recent issue that had cropped up within her grade level team. Since becoming the second-grade instructional team leader six years ago, she had experienced her share of concerns, but never one involving a key teacher on her team.

Michael Royal was the recent recipient of the Oakland Hills School District Teacher of the Year award. Handing out the award involved a rigorous and highly competitive process. Each year a committee consisting of parents, students, community leaders, and school-district employees bestowed this award for excellence in the profession to one deserving teacher. There was no doubt in anyone's mind that Mr. Royal, one of the school's family members, would eventually be noticed beyond the Oakland Hills community and would receive recognition as State Teacher of the Year. Hired 12 years previous, Michael had the respect of the entire community. A common occurrence was to have parents of first-grade students start a petition campaign, as early as spring, requesting that their child be placed in Mr. Royal's class for the upcoming fall. By all accounts, he was a superstar teacher from the start, keeping abreast of advanced teaching techniques and strategies by attending classes at the local university, as well as attending the professional development offerings provided by the district. Children not achieving academically elsewhere did so in Mr. Royal's classroom. In the past two years, parents pressured the principal to allow Mr. Royal to move through the grades with the same students until they left Blue Lakes Elementary School.

In addition to his skillful teaching abilities, Mr. Royal was charming and outgoing, leading to instant rapport with staff as well as parents. Often, teachers, students, and parents commented about how he brightened their day with his jokes, laughter, and contagious smile. He had an optimistic attitude about life in general that Janice counted on to brighten her days, as well.

However, that was not the case today, as Mrs. McRay thought about the conversation she had with another valued member of the school family, Mrs. Joy Su Li.

Joy Su: Hi, Janice. Do you have a minute?

Janice: Sure, come in and have a seat. What's on your mind, Joy Su?

Joy Su: Well, I don't know how to say this but . . .

Janice: But what?

Joy Su: I know you have so much on your mind and all and don't need one more thing to deal with . . .

Janice: It's okay. I am all ears. What's on your mind?

Joy Su: I just had a talk with Mike. We were putting up our bulletin boards together, and as you know, our theme this quarter is "Embracing and Celebrating Family." We thought it would be great if the teachers brought in pictures of their families and shared them with the students. Some of us have found our baby pictures and are going to display them in the hall. We are going to have a contest to see if the students can guess which baby picture belongs to whom.

Janice: *(Cutting into Joy Li's conversation)* Joy, I know all of this. What are you trying to tell me?

Joy Su: Well, when I was in Mike's room, I asked him where his family pictures were. He said that he was not going to bring pictures of his family, but would bring a baby picture for the contest. As you know, I knew him before he was hired at Blue Lakes. In fact, I told him about the position 12 years ago

and . . .

Janice: And what?

Joy Su: Well, there is no easy way to say this, but the reason he is not bringing his family pictures is because he does not think the school or district will embrace his family.

Janice: That's nonsense. We are very committed to family and so is the school system. Family has always been valued. Through all of the deaths, marriages, births, and divorces, we have all stuck together and supported one another. I can't imagine why Mike would think such a thing. Everyone on the staff showed up to celebrate his Teacher of the Year Award. I mean *everyone*. You know how difficult that can be with all of our busy schedules, but we made it happen because we all love and care about Mike. I will talk with him first thing in the morning and straighten this out.

Joy Su: Before you do, let me tell you why he said that he does not think the school or district wants him to display pictures of his family. He showed me pictures of his family. I was shocked, as I think you will be. As you know, he has two adopted sons . . . and . . . um . . . well . . . Michael is gay. His partner's name is Bill. The pictures of his family are of the four of them.

Janice sat in her chair stunned at the unsuspected information about the district's Teacher of the Year. She slumped in her chair, and put her hands over her forehead, paralyzed. What should she do with this new information? She thought, "Two years into the *inside-out* approach to change, the staff's 'family' is beginning to unravel."

Reflection

1. Who does the dominant culture serve in this case? Who is not served well by the dominant culture?

_____

_____

_____

_____

2. Janice McRay, Joy Su Li, and Michael Royal are ensnared by inconsistencies expressed around the value of family, resulting in internal conflict and disequilibrium. How might they regain balance around this value?

_____

_____

_____

_____

3. One of the fastest-growing criminal occurrences involves violent acts against gay and lesbian students. What are prevailing perspectives in this case that perpetuate this form of oppression?

_____

_____

_____

_____

4. What are your beliefs relative to this case? Given your values and beliefs, how would you approach this situation if you were Mike, Joy Su, or Janice?

_____

_____

_____

_____

5. Which Essential Element(s) applies to this situation and why (see Chapter 2)?

_____

_____

_____

_____

6 Barrier 2

Resistance to Change

Resistance to change is another of the three barriers to cultural proficiency. This barrier emanates from the perspective that change needs to happen as the result of others' actions, not by the actions of one's self. This barrier also recognizes that in many instances educators lack the awareness that they need to adapt. The language associated with this barrier typically refers to what "they" or "those" children or parents need to do rather that what "I" or "we" need to do for appropriate adjustments in meeting a challenge. As we discussed in Chapter 4, when teachers resist change, they have identified the parameters of their value system at the very edge of their lifeworld experience. They have no reference within the lifeworld experience to attach the situation in which they find themselves. They are in need of expanding their horizon experience for new reference points. Prior to reading the following two cases, review the questions Barbara Campbell prepared for Oakland Hills.

- How do the educators view their children and families? Do they describe the children as insiders or outsiders? For example, do they use pronouns such as "those" to describe children and families, viewing them as outsiders? Do educators use pronouns such as "our" to create an atmosphere of inclusion when describing students, families, and communities?
- Do educators critique their values and beliefs when addressing the needs of children and families?

CASE 3: SCIENCE LESSON

Ron Johnstone, principal of Eastside High, entered Noor Annous's classroom before the students arrived. He came to convey a complaint from a concerned parent about the subject matter she presented to her class. The parent, Mr. Adams, had leveled a charge that Ms. Annous was teaching racism to her students. Waving a copy of his son's homework assignment in the air, he demanded an immediate end to "the blatant racist practices of Ms. Annous."

Noor Annous, a science teacher at Eastside High School, started her career 19 years before at Westside High. Following several years of active recruitment by Mr. Johnstone, she transferred to Eastside High to teach students designated as a "more needy" area of the community by the Oakland Hills School District. Through the years, she worked with many promising students of which several had gone on to become contributors to national projects in the sciences. She was extremely proud of her career as a teacher. This year she was able to provide her students with a rather unique opportunity to study genetics by conducting laboratory experiments using samples of their mitochondrial DNA (mtDNA). Through this process, students could discover their genetic links to various groups in different geographic regions in the world. The students were extremely excited about discovering how they personally fit into the human genetic migratory map on the globe and eagerly engaged in the classroom experiments. Through this process, many made amazing discoveries of their genetic links that crossed known international and ethnic origins on the planet. She was surprised and appalled by the charge of racism made against her. She agreed to meet after school in Mr. Johnstone's office to discuss the matter in detail.

Two teachers, Bob Williams and Sanje Kosi, overheard a cell-phone conversation by Mr. Adams. He was discussing his situation with another party while standing in the parking lot after his meeting with the principal. Bob and Sanje were dissatisfied with Noor's teaching approach. They were among a prominent group of teachers advocating equal opportunity and access for students to learn given the students innate potential and aptitude to achieve. They supported tracking in their school because it allowed for those students with less innate ability to achieve at their own level. Therefore, they felt that the course Noor was teaching should be reserved for advanced-placement students who had the innate ability to handle the subject matter. Noor, in their opinion, was new to the school and tended to cross the line, going too far in helping *those* students with the subject matter. She was "too easy on those kids," they would comment off-handedly in the teacher's lounge. They seized this opportunity to approach the principal and make their point of view known about the new hire.

Once school was dismissed for the day, Noor went to the principal's office to discuss the parent's charge. Upon arriving, she met Bob Williams and Sanje Kosi leaving Mr. Johnstone's office. They politely greeted Noor as they crossed paths in the office hallway. Feeling a bit uncomfortable, Noor entered the office and sat down in a chair offered to her by Ron Johnstone across from his desk. Shortly after, Mr. Adams arrived and sat alongside the principal's desk. She recognized Mr. Adams as the parent of one of her most promising students.

After somewhat cordial greetings, Mr. Adams got right to the point. Placing a sheet of paper (see Figure 6.1) on the principal's desk, he sternly objected to the content of the subject matter on the paper. After making several points, he concluded by stating that there was no place for racism in America's schools, especially reverse racism. "We are a color-blind society and I would like to keep it that way," he stated emphatically.

Noor reached over and gathered the paper from Mr. Johnstone's desk. She quickly recognized it as the list of key points she wanted her students to understand about the concept of race versus color. Many students were initially confused about concepts of color in human gene expression and their understanding of race. As a part of the laboratory experiment with their own mtDNA, they were able to understand how the concept of race had no biological basis, particularly as it relates to human gene expression. The students began to understand race as a social political construct designed for the benefit of some, at the expense of others. Color, on the other hand, was nature's way of naturally selecting the appropriate amount of melanin (dark pigmentation) in the skin for the survival of the human species' migration from Sub-Saharan Africa across continents populating the planet.

With great effort, Noor explained the lesson to Mr. Adams. However, he rejected her argument regardless of all scientific explanations she gave him. The final straw in the conversation came when she mentioned how the students were learning to be independent researchers and that Joseph, Mr. Adam's son, was most promising in this area. At that point, Mr. Adams stood up and angrily left the office. Stunned, Noor looked at Ron Johnstone, who had sat quietly throughout the meeting.

Figure 6.1   10 Things Everybody Should Know About Race

1. Race is a modern idea. Ancient societies, like the Greeks, did not divide people according to physical differences, but according to religion, status, class, or even language. The English word "race" turns up for the first time in a 1508 poem by William Dunbar referring to a line of kings.

2. Race has no genetic basis. Not one characteristic, trait, or even gene distinguishes all the members of one so-called race from all the members of another so-called race.

3. Human subspecies don't exist. Unlike many animals, modern humans simply haven't been around long enough, nor have populations been isolated enough, to evolve into separate subspecies or races. On average, only one of every thousand of the nucleotides that make up our DNA differ one human from another. We are one of the most genetically similar of all species.

(Continued)

Figure 6.1 (Continued)

4. Skin color really is only skin deep. The genes for skin color have nothing to do with genes for hair form, eye shape, blood type, musical talent, athletic ability, or forms of intelligence. Knowing someone's skin color doesn't necessarily tell you anything else about him or her.

5. Most variation is within, not between, "races." Of the small amount of total human variation, 85% exists within any local population. About 94% can be found within any continent. That means, for example, that two random Koreans may be as genetically different as a Korean and an Italian.

6. Slavery predates race. Throughout much of human history, societies have enslaved others, often as a result of conquest or debt, but not because of physical characteristics or a belief in natural inferiority. Due to a unique set of historical circumstances, North America had the first slave system where all slaves shared a common appearance and ancestry.

7. Race and freedom were born together. The United States was founded on the principle that "All men are created equal," but the country's early economy was based largely on slavery. The new idea of race helped explain why some people could be denied the rights and freedoms that others took for granted.

8. Race justified social inequalities as natural. The "common sense" belief in white superiority justified antidemocratic action and policies like slavery, the extermination of American Indians, the exclusion of Asian immigrants, the taking of Mexican lands, and the institutionalization of racial practices within American government, laws, and society.

9. Race isn't biological, but racism is still real. Race is a powerful social idea that gives people different access to opportunities and resources. The government and social institutions of the United States have created advantages that disproportionately channel wealth, power, and resources to white people.

10. Colorblindness will not end racism. Pretending race doesn't exist is not the same as creating equality.

SOURCE: From the documentary series *Race—The Power of an Illusion*. Available from California Newsreel at www.newsreel.org.

Reflection

1. What do you think Noor Annous's values are as they pertain to teaching students? How do her values compare/contrast to the ones you have identified in Chapter 3?

_____

_____

_____

_____

2. Bob Williams and Sanje Kosi are prominent voices on staff at the school. They are resistant to the idea of some of Noor's students becoming independent thinkers. What do you think are their values and beliefs that support this resistance?

_____

_____

_____

_____

3. According to Sergiovanni's rules of motivation in Chapter 4, Table 4.1, people's motivations are classified as calculated (what gets rewarded gets done), intrinsic (what is rewarding gets done), or moral (what is good gets done). How would you classify each of the characters' *involvement* in the case:

Bob Williams and Sanje Kosi, teachers

_____

Noor Annous, science teacher

_____

Ron Johnstone, principal

_____

Mr. Adams, parent

_____

4. What do you suppose is Ron Johnstone's resistance to speaking up in the meeting with Noor and Mr. Adams? What does Ron Johnstone value?

_____

_____

_____

_____

5. What guiding principles are operational in this case? Describe an aspect of the dominant culture of the school as demonstrated by the principal, Bob, and Sanje. Amongst the characters in Question 3, who is served well and who is not?

_____

_____

_____

_____

6. Which of the Essential Elements can be used to help the principal, Bob, and Sanje overcome their resistance? How would you use the elements you identify? How do your core beliefs square with the actions of the principal, teachers, and parent in the case?

_____

_____

_____

_____

7. Identify three of the parent's (Mr. Adams) behaviors. On which points of the continuum do they each fall? Who should be responsible to help him move forward on the continuum? Why do you believe as you do?

_____

_____

_____

_____

8. Given CampbellJones' model in Chapter 4 of intentional moral action, what must Noor do to remain congruent with her values and beliefs in the Eastside High School culture?

_____

_____

_____

_____

9. Think of a situation in your school, district, or organization where the culture did not serve you well. What values and beliefs did you hold that were not supported in that culture?

_____

_____

_____

_____

10. Think of a situation in your school, district, or organization where the culture served you well. What values and beliefs did you hold that were

congruent with the values and beliefs of the organization? As a member of that dominant culture, what changes in that culture, if any, no longer served you well? What caused you to resist? How did it feel?

_____

_____

_____

_____

CASE 4: PUBLIC ANNOUNCEMENT

Kevin Bullock has been principal of Twin Valley Middle School for the past five years. He has learned a great deal in this position, most of which was about himself. He has become increasingly aware of his values and beliefs and how they shape his actions. Kevin was also keenly aware of the influence he had over others and sought opportunities to influence those with whom he worked.

During his five-year tenure as principal, there was a shift in the student population at Twin Valley. The number of students with Asian backgrounds had grown each of the five years by 3% each year. Overall, students of Korean background now comprised 5% of the population. Students from India totaled 2% and 3% were of Chinese origin. Additionally, there was an influx of students from the Middle East making up 2% of the school population. The remainder of the student population was comprised of 10% African-American and 78% Euro-American.

As principal, Kevin considered what he should do to make transitions easier for students who were new to the school. One student, in particular, came to Kevin's mind: his name was Harpreet Singh. He was new to Twin Valley, and received services from the English for Speakers of Other Languages office. He wore a turban when no one else did. From watching the news, Kevin was well aware of instances in the community involving the harassment of people from South Asia. He was also aware of the dominant culture at Twin Valley and suspected that Harpreet was most likely having a difficult time transitioning into the school culture.

The Martin Luther King holiday was quickly approaching. Kevin thought this observance was a great opportunity to welcome Harpreet into the Twin Valley school community. The school had spent a great deal of time preparing for Black History Month, which soon followed the King holiday. This, he reasoned, would provide the perfect context for responding to the growing differences at Twin Valley.

On the school day prior to the observance of Martin Luther King's birthday, Kevin eagerly anticipated the afternoon announcements. He carefully constructed a statement and waited to read it to the entire Twin Valley school community over the school public announcement system. At 2:55 P.M., he began the usual afternoon announcements. He saved this portion of his address until the very end—a final thought before sending the students home for a long weekend.

> Students, this Monday we will observe Dr. Martin Luther King's birthday. On this day, it is important to reflect upon the message of Dr. King. We need to remember to judge all people by the content of their character, not by other things, such as the color of their skin, their clothing, or their religion. For example, although Muslims might believe in violence, that does not mean we should judge all Muslims. I want you to have a great weekend, and spend some time on Monday thinking about how we can all be a little bit more like Dr. King.

The following Tuesday, Kevin received a phone call from Mrs. Farida Mohammadi, a concerned parent, who requested a meeting before the day's end. Kevin cleared his calendar and scheduled the meeting with her. Later that day, after students left the building, Kevin gladly greeted Mrs. Mohammadi in the front reception area and politely escorted her to his office.

Farida: Thank you for meeting with me so soon after my request.

Kevin: Sure. It's important to me that our school is responsive to our students and community. Now, let's discuss your concern.

Farida: I must first tell you that I am uncomfortable bringing this topic to you.

Kevin: Please, let me assure you that what you have to say is very important to me.

Farida: *(Sighing)* Yes. My son came home in tears on Friday because of something that you said on the announcements. He said that you announced that Muslims believe in violence.

Kevin: That is not what I said.

Farida: Well, I have to say that I did not believe him at first. I told him that he must have misunderstood the announcements. He must not have heard you correctly. However, later that evening, I received a phone call from a friend who is also Muslim. She asked if I had heard about the announcement. Then I spoke with another parent who heard the same thing from her child. Both verified my son's story. I feel horrible that I doubted him.

Kevin: Allow me to explain. We have a new student this year. He wears a turban, and I did not want other students harassing him.

Farida: I know that student. He is actually a Sikh, not a Muslim.

Kevin: *(Leaning back in his chair)* I am not sure that I know the difference. Perhaps you can explain it to me later. Thank you for telling me about this. However, you are the only person who has brought this up as an issue. In fact, this morning I had a student thank me for making the announcement. I think the Muslim students appreciated what I was saying.

Farida: I believe that many students and parents were offended. Many parents will not come forward, however. They do not want to risk damaging their relationships with the school. But, I think this is too important and must be addressed. Muslims are misrepresented in the media, and it has been extraordinarily difficult for us since 9/11. Students should feel valued in school, not misrepresented or stereotyped by their own teachers and administrators.

Kevin: I agree. What would you like me to do?

Farida: I would like you to address this openly and honestly. The Parent Teachers Association (PTA) meeting is tomorrow night. That would be a good start.

After Mrs. Mohammadi departed, Kevin thought about the meeting. What could he possibly say? He was aware that he did not know much about Muslims, except for what he saw on the news. Should he admit his ignorance to the parent community? Should he downplay Mrs. Mohammadi's concern? He was also aware of the overriding attitudes of several prominent members of the PTA, especially Jean Rogers, the president. Jean was very upset about the new mosque built near her home. Since its construction, traffic congestion during hours of worship had become unbearable. Jean had forcefully spoken out against constructing the mosque during public hearings at the city council meeting. Before Jean's arrival to the school as a parent, the PTA was dysfunctional and had little impact in the school. She single-handedly revitalized the organization and turned it into a significant force in school/community affairs. Kevin sat in his office alone thinking about his options.

Reflection

1. What is Kevin's dilemma? Given the request to present this issue to the PTA, what recommendations do you have for Kevin?

_____

_____

_____

_____

2. Kevin wants to do well. However, Kevin's description of Muslims contributes to his conundrum. On which point(s) of the continuum would his afternoon announcement comment fall? Select one of his comments and rewrite it so that it is a culturally competent comment.

_____

_____

_____

_____

3. How does his language support the Barriers to Cultural Proficiency?

_____

_____

_____

_____

4. What Cultural Proficiency Principle(s) would you employ as a guide in advising him? Why?

_____

_____

_____

_____

5. Which Essential Element should Kevin use in approaching this dilemma? How will this essential element help?

_____

_____

_____

_____

6. Why do you suppose Mrs. Mohammadi and other parents hesitate to approach Kevin Bullock? What assumptions are they making?

_____

_____

_____

_____

LEFT HAND/RIGHT HAND: DRILLING DEEPER

As principal, Kevin Bullock was compelled to respond positively to the students coming to Twin Valley Middle School. He was acutely sensitive to the different cultural values and norms that new students brought to the school environment. He did not want to ignore their differences and act as if they did not exist. Yet it was clear to him that he was lacking the skills needed to be effective in achieving this objective. By measures of the Cultural Proficiency Continuum, Kevin was precompetent with this issue.

He had spoken with the superintendent of Oakland Hills School District, Ed Soriano. Dr. Soriano suggested that he make an appointment with Barbara Campbell to coach him through his situation. Kevin was open to suggestions and promptly made the appointment. They agreed to meet in Kevin's office. The following dialogue (in Table 6.1) captures their conversation. It also highlights Barbara's thought process as she coaches Kevin through his dilemma. The conversation is presented in the format of "left hand/right hand" columns (Argyris, 1990). The left-hand column tracks Barbara Campbell's thoughts while in conversation with Kevin. We get an inside view of her application of the tools of cultural proficiency, as well as other organizational dynamic applications she has in her arsenal. The right-hand column tracks the spoken conversation between the two of them.

Table 6.1 Left Hand/Right Hand

Left Hand (Things thought by Barbara, but not said aloud.)	**Right Hand** (Things spoken aloud by Kevin and Barbara.)
From my notes and in my meeting with Dr. Soriano, I anticipate this will be a productive meeting. I assume Kevin wants my assistance and is genuinely interested in applying the Principles of Cultural Proficiency to his work.	*Kevin:* Dr. Campbell, thanks for agreeing to meet with me. As you know from our discussion on the telephone, I have a bit of a dilemma here.
	Barbara: I can see that somewhat. Just for clarity, give me a little bit more information. Where do you feel caught?
Kevin acknowledges several principles of cultural proficiency. He recognizes differences in the school population (Principle 3); he surfaces the idea that there is a dominant culture (Principle 1); and he questions how well the different groups are being served by the dominant culture (Principle 2).	*Kevin:* Truthfully, I don't want to go into the PTA meeting and cause a conflict. We have worked very hard to bring this school together. We enroll new students every quarter and they are coming from different countries around the world. We also have a core of families that have been in this community for three generations.
	Barbara: Let's take these one at a time. The predominant culture here has at least three generations of tradition. How would you characterize this culture—the values, beliefs, and norms?
	Kevin: Wow, that is a little bit tough. If I picked three prevailing values, I would choose respect, honesty, generosity. I think folks feel that a person should be respectful at all cost, should be honest in their dealings, and strive to be generous to others regardless of who the other person happens to be.
How can I help Kevin address the values and beliefs acknowledged and practiced by members of the different groups in his school? The way to manage any perceived conflict arising out of differences (Essential Element 3—Managing the Dynamics of Difference) that does not incapacitate or become destructive is to focus the conversation with healthy processes that allow values to surface (Cultural Proficiency Continuum; Ladder of Inference).	*Barbara:* How are these values and beliefs normalized? What are the observable actions that tell you that people in the school and community actually practice these values on a regular basis?
	Kevin: Well, I see students helping each other in the schoolyard. Parents also assist each other with their children. I believe that is one of the reasons the PTA is gaining momentum. In fact, they have organized a rainy-day fund for some families that are newcomers to the community to help them adjust.

Left Hand (Things thought by Barbara, but not said aloud.)	Right Hand (Things spoken aloud by Kevin and Barbara.)
It is clear that members of the community are well intentioned. However, there seems to be an undercurrent of an unawareness of the need to adapt given that the population is shifting. This could lead to the barrier "Resistance to Change" pitting groups against each other. Kevin needs to find common ground between the groups. The most stable place of common ground is in identifying common values.	*Barbara:* I assume this fund extends to all newcomers, or is it solely families that look and act like the core community that has been here for three generations?

Kevin: Well, it is set up to assist all newcomers. To be truthful, it has only been used for a few families and those families seem to "fit in" well with the folks that are already here.

Barbara: And the families that do not "fit in"?

Kevin: I see your point. Maybe the core community has the value of respect, honesty, and generosity, but is not practicing it fully?

Barbara: There, you have made a connection. I think a good point you could make in the PTA meeting is your attempt to build upon something that is valued in the core community—respect, honesty, and generosity—and that your announcement was an attempt at practicing those values. However, you openly and honestly admit that it has been brought to your attention that you did not do so well with the public announcement. |
| Can Kevin assess the school community (Essential Element 1—Assessing Cultural Knowledge) to see if there are common values held by different groups? He can then work purposefully to help them find common actions. | *Kevin:* I think this works. By acknowledging their values, it gives everyone permission to be included. I never looked at it that way before.

Barbara: Now for the larger question. What about the newcomers? Do you see their values as being the same as those of the core community?

Kevin: Well, now that I think about it, yes. I see each group being respectful to others, there is a great deal of honesty, and I have seen many occasions of open generosity.

Barbara: This becomes your platform to help the groups stitch things together. Although they might show their values in different ways, they have them in common nonetheless. Your challenge will be to help them see how the actions of each group is an expression of the same set of values and how over time they can come together with common actions.

Kevin: I think I can do that. |

Reflection

1. What do you think are Kevin's primary beliefs (principles by which he lives)? How do these guide him in his actions to serve the families in the school?

_____

_____

_____

_____

2. Think of Brenda CampbellJones' model of Intentional Moral Action in Chapter 4. What is causing Kevin's disequilibrium? What kind of experiences does he need to help him see what he can't see? Upon what does he need to reflect?

_____

_____

_____

_____

3. How did Barbara Campbell assist him in gaining balance?

_____

_____

_____

_____

7 Barrier 3

A Sense of Privilege and Entitlement

A sense of privilege and entitlement arises from indifference to benefits that accrue solely by one's membership in a gender, race, or other cultural group. This barrier encapsulates the practice of denying one group's societal benefits while awarding those same benefits to others. It recognizes that benefits gained by the dominant group accrue over time and pass from one generation to the next. For example, denying you the right to vote essentially gives me two votes—mine and the one denied you. Likewise, the same applies to educational advancement in schools. It is common to see historically oppressed populations of children—African American, Latino, and Native American—clustered in low-level academic courses while upper-level courses are filled with historically advantaged groups, primarily Euro-American. The clear distribution of academic benefits for Whites and lack thereof for people of color is evident in the achievement data reported over the past two decades (NAEP 2007; The Educational Trust, 2006).

Key questions associated with this barrier include:

- Are there practices or policies in place that serve one group better than another? Are certain families served better than others? Are schools in one zip code served better than schools in another?
- Do some groups purposefully have unfair advantages over others? What beliefs support this practice?
- Do new teachers get the least support? Are they forced to move from room to room, due to space issues, while veteran teachers stay in a single room? Do veteran teachers get their choice of students? What are the underlying values that support these practices?

CASE 5: HEART CONDITION

The staff at Wondering Wood Elementary School has spent the past two years working with the tools of cultural proficiency. The demographics of the school have changed little over the past 10 years. White students comprise over 80% of the school population. For decades, the school maintained deeply rooted traditions and practices. It was through their work with cultural proficiency that the staff realized that they must engage and adapt their practice in order to fulfill their mission: Prepare students for successful participation in a diverse and changing world.

This was a paradigm shift—a fundamental switch in the way they saw things. Many had previously believed that adaptation was necessary when responding to diversity *within* the school. Now there was a sense that the staff must change practices in order to respond to the diverse global community that students would experience upon leaving the school. Jane Simmons, school principal, committed herself to helping the staff grow from the *inside-out* in order to fulfill the promise of their mission. She believed that each staff member would work to *be* the change they wished to see in the world.

Jane questioned her beliefs the December day that Ross Dewey, parent of a new fourth-grade student, Reid, entered her office for the second time. In an earlier meeting, Mr. Dewey alerted Ms. Simmons about his son's heart condition and his need for accommodations in Reid's physical education class. Thanking Mr. Dewey for the advanced notice, Jane assured the father that his son would receive proper care for a successful experience at Wondering Woods Elementary. However, during this meeting, the father raised the question as to what a successful and caring experience really looked like for his son. Mr. Dewey conveyed that Reid's experience in the class was very demeaning, even to the point where it was causing behavioral problems at home. "We noticed that he came home on Thursdays after school in a very bad mood. When we finally challenged him on the issue, he burst into tears and vowed not to go back to the class." When pressed by the principal as to the reasons for the changed behavior, Mr. Dewey said, "He finally told us that he feels like a failure in P.E. He told us that Mr. Eckstein, his teacher, yells at him and even puts him down with little jokes in front of the whole class. You know, he calls him a 'slow-poke' for always being the last one to line up."

Mr. Dewey finished his comments by stating that he tried without success to talk with Mr. Eckstein, but the teacher became defensive in their conversations. Mr. Eckstein's response was that he treated all the kids the same and all the other students felt fine with him "joking" around with them because it was his personality to joke around with the students.

"It's just that jokes that put people down, and particularly Reid, aren't funny to him," Mr. Dewey stated passionately. "They're demeaning to who he is. The final straw for me took place last week. Reid told me that he asked to return to his locker to get his jacket. He said that Mr. Eckstein yelled at him for talking out of turn and made him sit against the gymnasium wall for the remainder of class."

Mrs. Simmons assured him that the school had Reid's best interest at heart. She said that she would meet with Mr. Eckstein and get to the bottom of Mr. Dewey's concern. Before he left her office, she scheduled a follow-up meeting.

Later that week, Jane Simmons, Ross Dewey, and Sean Eckstein met. The meeting took place after school in the principal's office, as Sean would not meet during his planning hour, citing his contractual rights. Jane began the meeting by summarizing the situation, the father's concerns, and the purpose of the meeting—to resolve this conflict. She was careful to mention the student's physical needs and cite the school's mission to prepare students for successful participation in a diverse and changing world. However, it did not take long before the meeting began to deteriorate.

Sean: If Reid would just follow directions, these types of things wouldn't happen. Plus, he's always asking to leave class. It wasn't just the jacket incident. It's the need to go to the water fountain, the bathroom; leaving the classroom to get something he forgot; heading to the office to make phone calls; needing to talk with the nurse. The list goes on and on. He needs to learn responsibility, respect, and preparation.

Ross: I think, at this point, Reid might be trying to find ways to get out of class because he doesn't feel good about himself when he's in class.

Sean: Look, I've been doing this for 23 years. I should know what I'm talking about.

Jane: I think we should focus on how to help Reid experience success and feel as if he's included in the P.E. class and activities.

Sean: But he obviously doesn't like physical activities. How can someone be involved in things when they don't even want to be there?

Ross: He *does* like physical activities. He has a physically limiting condition and needs some accommodation so he can successfully participate. He feels belittled by you and that's the reason he doesn't want to be there.

Sean: Look, I've taught here my entire career and have never been criticized like this. I don't appreciate what you're insinuating, and I don't have anything else to share. As far as I'm concerned, this meeting is over. I am not the problem here. That kid needs to learn to adjust if he is going be successful in life.

At that point, Sean Eckstein stood up, pushed his chair aside, and left the room. Jane looked into the eyes of Ross Dewey, as he sat with his arms folded. She thought about Sean Eckstein and how he, along with the rest of the staff, had committed to cultural proficiency. Yet how could the school meet Reid Dewey's needs, given the result of the meeting?

Reflection

1 Through the lens of cultural proficiency, the person(s) in the power position should take responsibility to respond in a competent manner. Mr. Eckstein stated that he had worked as a physical education teacher for 23 years. Given his privilege and entitlement in that situation, what could he have done to respond in a competent or proficient way to the parent and the student?

_____

_____

_____

_____

2. What are the underlying values and beliefs in the mission statement "Prepare students for successful participation in a diverse and changing world." What are Mr. Eckstein's values, as depicted in this case? How are his expressed values in conflict with the values you have identified in the mission?

_____

_____

_____

_____

3. How might privilege and entitlement thwart the staff's efforts in truly realizing their espoused mission statement? How might the principal help Mr. Eckstein to see how his sense of entitlement, in this situation, is preventing him from responding in a proficient manner?

_____

_____

_____

_____

4. Revisit the conversation in the principal's office. List several of the statements made by any of the characters. What values are expressed in those statements? Where on the continuum does each statement fall?

_____

_____

_____

_____

5. Using the essential element Managing the Dynamics of Difference, how would you move the conversation by Mr. Eckstein, Ross Dewey, and Jane Simmons from unhealthy to healthy, as indicated on the Cultural Proficiency Continuum? How could you use this essential element to diminish the sense of privilege and entitlement, thus leveling the playing field?

_____

_____

_____

_____

6. Consider a time when you were in the power position (teacher-to-student, parent-to-child, principal-to-teacher, superintendent-to-principal, etc.) and the less powerful person in the relationship demanded a change. Did you respond in a competent or proficient way? Why or why not? What strategies did you use to overcome any defensiveness you may have experienced? How did you level the playing field with regard to your privilege/entitlement?

_____

_____

_____

_____

CASE 6: EARLY AMERICA

Ever since the study of Colonial America became part of the sixth-grade curriculum, Edward Middle School has held a "Sixth-Grade Early American Day" event. Throughout the course of the day, students rotate from classroom to classroom, simulating different Early American colonial-era activities. Families and community members attend the day, often holding camcorders to capture memories for a lifetime. Schoolwide staff members such as art, music, and physical-education teachers design activities and/or dress to support the day. Frequently, former students cite the event as one of their favorite memories when they reflect upon experiences at Edward Middle School. It has become a tradition that students eagerly anticipate as they progress through the grades.

Each year, the sixth-grade teachers send an announcement in the form of a flyer home with students, communicating the nature of the event and inviting community attendance. This year, like in years past, the flyer read:

Dressing for Early American Day

On Friday, our sixth graders will celebrate Early America! The day will be full of activities that are a culmination of our unit on Colonial America. Students are encouraged to dress as a trade person or citizen in Colonial America. Parents are invited and we strongly encourage your attendance.

What made this year different from past events is that after sending home the flyer, for the first time, the sixth-grade teachers received critical feedback from a parent of one of the students. It arrived through e-mail.

Dear Sixth-Grade Teachers,

Overall, my husband and I have been pleased with our childrens' experience at Edward Middle. As you know, our older son Greg enjoyed his year in sixth grade. This year, our other son Kyle loves coming to school and we thank you for providing a nurturing environment.

The purpose of this e-mail is to bring your attention to our concerns about the upcoming Early American Day. I am cc'ing the principal because I am aware that this may have administrative implications. Two years ago, Greg participated in the event, and at the time I did wonder how the African American experience would be portrayed to the students in the school. Nevertheless, I put no further thought into it and took no action at that time.

However, last night when Kyle brought home the "Dressing for Early America Day" flyer, he asked me if he should dress up as a *slave* for the event. I told him that I was proud of him for asking such a good question and for being concerned about his history.

I would never send my son to school dressed as a slave. Thus, this situation does raise the issue of how—and if—African American life is being handled within this event. As I'm sure you are aware, almost the entire African American population was legally enslaved during the Colonial period. Although some African American men learned a trade, most were slaves.

We are certainly not against the Early American Day event. However, we do believe that for this event to be accurate and authentic, you must consider the issue of slavery. What we feel needs to be considered above all is the impact of the event on African American students and the authenticity of history for all children at Edward Middle. Please feel free to contact me regarding this issue.

Regards,
Cheryl Edmond, Parent

Her message triggered a quick e-mail reply from the sixth-grade teacher team leader, Mr. Todd Sanders. Todd took great care to provide details about the overall curriculum leading up to the event with the intent of assuring Mrs. Edmond that the children at Edward Middle received the best education possible.

Dear Mrs. Edmond,

Thank you for your e-mail and for opening a discussion on an important component of our nation's history. As I see it, your concern is with how African American history during Colonial times (slavery in particular) is being addressed by both our Early American Day event and our classroom instruction in general. Allow me to explain.

We base the Early American Day event on one of the chapters in our social studies textbook. It describes life in Colonial Williamsburg and includes the African American experience, in an appropriate manner, as part of the chapter. One of our activities is focused on this. Students learn that about half of the population of Williamsburg were enslaved Africans. They then learn about their jobs, how difficult conditions often were, and how African Americans relied on each other, their culture, and of course, their spiritual beliefs to endure such conditions.

Earlier in our unit of study, students read an entire chapter dedicated to the African experience related to the development of the American colonies. They learn about West African culture, the effects of European slave trade, and the dilemmas of Africa as other Africans were enslaved. We teach them about the inhumane conditions of the Middle Passage, as well as how enslaved Africans experienced harsh conditions once they reached the Americas.

I do not doubt that Kyle asked his question about his dress for this event because of the pride you have instilled about your children's history and character, as well as his exposure to the above-mentioned curriculum. I assure you the most qualified scholars in the field prepare this unit of study. It is widely used throughout the country as one of the best units on this subject.

Please feel free to contact me without hesitation should you have other questions or concerns.

Thank you.

Todd Sanders
Sixth-Grade Team Leader

Mrs. Edmond received the message and in an effort to have her voice heard and clarify her concern, promptly responded that same day.

Mr. Sanders,

Thank you for your response about how the African American experience is part of the social studies curriculum. Of course, its inclusion in American history is a given due to slavery's impact on Colonial times and America in general.

However, I do not think you understood my primary concern. The fact that you ask students to "dress up" for Early American Day is disconcerting. Your African American students are well aware that they would have been slaves—not tradespeople or Colonial "citizens," as the flyer that was sent home suggests—during that time period. Actually, I am sure that all of your students surely understand this. It is my belief that this is what prompted Kyle's question.

My hope is that you understand how "dressing up" for this event is awkward for African American students, and possibly other "nonwhite" students as well. Given the tremendous amount of diversity at Edward Middle, I believe that dressing up is not appropriate, nor is it necessary, to learning about the colonial period.

In regard to Early American Day, I simply would like the Edward Middle School staff to consider the perspectives of *all* of their students. Consider their backgrounds. Consider their feelings. Consider them before assuming that everyone is okay with dressing up as a European American colonist.

I hope that you give some serious thought to my perspective on this issue. Although I can only speak for myself and my family, I am positive that other parents feel this way and simply have not expressed it.

Sincerely,
Cheryl Edmond, Parent

The series of e-mails clearly points to a conflict in differences about the Early American Day event. Although her older son participated in the event and, based upon her own testimony, enjoyed the affair, Cheryl Edmond is clearly disturbed about the overall effects the event might have on Kyle and indeed both children. Consider the mother's circumstance. If she chooses not to send the e-mail to alert the school of the damaging effect of this day on the psyche of her African American child primarily and all children in general, she risks a major violation of a deeply held belief—the protection of her child and indeed other children. However, by sending the e-mail she may also risk placing her child in jeopardy of possible retribution from his teachers, thus violating the same value of protecting her child. Cheryl Edmond is squarely in a dilemma.

But she is not alone. The school also faces a conundrum. Dr. Darian Monroe, the principal at Edward Middle, studied the e-mail exchange and thought it best to intervene. He offered to meet with Mrs. Edmond. She gladly accepted with hopes of shedding light on the situation. The following was part of their conversation.

Dr. Monroe: Thank you for your time. As you know, one of our main goals at Edward Middle is that every student feels safe and nurtured. I want to do whatever I can to make sure that we achieve this goal for Kyle.

Mrs. Edmond: Thank you. We love this school, and as I mentioned before, I am not against Early American Day. My intention was neither to cause a major situation nor to draw any unpleasant attention toward Kyle. When Kyle asked me if he should dress as a slave, it broke my heart. Honestly, at this point, I would just like to fade off into the background. I've stated my concerns clearly and simply, and would appreciate it if the sixth-grade team consider my thoughts as they plan the event.

Dr. Monroe: Would you like me to get the curriculum office at the central office involved? I could contact the coordinator of social studies and explain the situation. Perhaps the curriculum should change. What are you thoughts?

Mrs. Edmond: No, I don't want that kind of power. I don't know enough about the appropriate curriculum to make those kinds of recommendations.

Dr. Monroe: I understand. I'm going to meet with the sixth-grade team tomorrow to discuss this situation. They are a responsive and responsible group—the best in the district—and I know that they will do what is right for students. I also wanted to inform you about Cultural Proficiency, one of our school district's major initiatives. The entire district is committed to becoming a culturally proficient organization. This year, we have assembled a cultural proficiency team of 10 staff members who are participating in ongoing seminars to gain awareness on the approach and apply it to our school. Do you mind if I share this situation with members of the staff and district?

Mrs. Edmond: Of course. It is great to hear that the school and the district are committed to equity. Please let the team know that this is a *real* situation with real people, feelings, and consequences. Also, I appreciate your involvement with the sixth-grade team. Please keep me informed about what takes place.

The next day, Dr. Darian Monroe met with the sixth-grade team, one day prior to Early American Day. He wanted to convey Mrs. Edmond's concerns from the conference held the previous day. He was on a first-name basis with team members and felt confident they would be open to hearing her concerns. Present were Todd Sanders, Joy Cockrell, Tracy Garvey, and Sherry Johnson.

Darian: I met with Mrs. Edmond. She is not angry with you, nor does she want Early American Day stopped. She is, however, concerned about how our invitation for students to "dress colonial" is received by our "nonwhite" students.

Joy: Well, it would be a shame to ruin a great tradition and experience for the students just because of one concern. We've been having this event for as long as I've worked here, and everyone loves it. So do I. The kids are so cute when they come to school all dressed up. I would hate for that to end. I just want what is best for our students.

Sherry: Besides, we're not asking the students to dress as their ancestors would have dressed. We're asking them to dress as citizens and tradesmen would have dressed in Early-American times.

Todd: Hold on. It doesn't sound like Mrs. Edmond wants us to end our tradition. I think I see her concern. When she first wrote to us, I couldn't believe that what we did every year could have caused a family such distress. I think we may want to think about changing the wording on our flyer to make it more inclusive. I think we need to demonstrate that we serve all of our students.

Tracy: Well, there's nothing we can do now. The event is tomorrow, and I have all of my materials printed and my parent volunteers lined up.

Darian: That's true. Mrs. Edmond does not want to make this a big deal. At first, I was concerned that this situation was going to explode. Her main concern, however, is dress for the day. We may want to consider this for next year. Let's go ahead with tomorrow as planned.

The sixth-grade team has a dilemma of competing commitments. They value their instructional program and take pride in what they consider to be a successful tradition—Early American Day. However, they value the well being of each student and, with the new information given them by Cheryl Edmond, they are clearly in violation of this value.

Reflection

1. Consider the school's choice to go ahead with the day as planned. Was this the *right* decision? Why? Why not? Which of your values and beliefs drives your reason?

_____

_____

_____

_____

2. Who benefits from this decision to have the event? Who does not? Why? Why not?

_____

_____

_____

_____

3. What possible historical legacies of entitlement and privilege does Early American Day perpetuate?

_____

_____

_____

_____

4. How are all students affected by participating in Early American Day, as it is currently constructed? What implications are there for curriculum and instruction?

_____

_____

_____

_____

5. How would you respond if you were:

The parent?

A member of the sixth grade team?

The principal?

_____

_____

_____

_____

6. Revisit the beliefs inventory you took in Chapter 3. Selecting the one(s) with the lowest score (5 and below), how can you strengthen it using what you have learned?

_____

_____

_____

_____

7. Are you questioning any of your values? If so, which ones, and why?

_____

_____

_____

_____

Heuristic Reflection

Who hath a greater combat than he that laboreth to overcome himself? This ought to be our endeavor, to conquer ourselves, and daily to wax stronger. . . .

—Kempis, 1980, p. 29

A fundamental premise of this book is that we, as educators, must change in order to provide high academic education for each child. Through Cultural Proficiency, we seek an *inside-out* transformational approach to change for educators. A change of this kind highlights a fundamental shift in moral perspective. For most educators this shift is paradigmatic, requiring a complete makeover of fundamental beliefs about how teachers and school leaders view their relationships with students and their families. This shift causes us to explore a greater vision:

- Imagine an educational system where every educator had courage of their convictions to do what is right on behalf of their students and families.
- Imagine practicing culturally competent behaviors and advocating on behalf of students in situations where an adult was clearly destructive toward children.
- Imagine a culture where educators are open and honest enough to admit they did not have the skills to teach *every* child and were willing to learn to do so in a culturally proficient manner.
- Imagine an educational system where each individual followed the moral mandates of their hearts rather than following legislated mandates.
- Imagine an educational system that operated from a position of faith and confidence rather than fear.

- Imagine an educational system where every cultural group is esteemed and people are eagerly seeking alliances with groups other than their own.

If you can imagine it, you can believe it. If you can believe it, you can eventually bring it to fruition. In this book, we introduced you to ideas, constructs, and processes designed to assist with that task as well as inform your morality. Framed within the context of Cultural Proficiency, you have tools that are used successfully by members of school communities in North America to reshape their moral compass toward educating every student to achieve high academic standards rather than the traditional view of only educating those who we fondly term "the best and brightest." In light of the No Child Left Behind Act of 2001 (NCLB), the stakes are higher dictating that educators not leave children behind.

While it is true that government has played a key role in shaping the histories of various groups of people in conflicting relationship to that of the dominant culture, government cannot legislate morality (King, 1998). After numerous lower court rulings, Supreme Court decisions, legislative mandates, and executive orders, it is clear that these governmental constructs are unable to bring about societal equality overnight. In fact, these governmental branches were in many cases the prime forces for creating and maintaining disparities among the American citizenry (Low & Clift, 1981). However, even with the best intentions of court rulings, executive orders, and legislative mandates such as NCLB, we will continue to leave children behind if educators do not value moving them forward.

Our hope is that after reading this book, you realize the powerful role educators play in the socialization of society from one generation to the next. True change comes about one person at a time and within the collective "we" society tips toward transformation. Minimally, you should be disturbed enough to reflect upon your personal values and beliefs and those of your school and district. It should be clear to you the direct link between what you value, what you assume, and how your assumptions shape what you believe to be true. Ultimately, your actions spring from your beliefs of what you assume to be true.

After reading this book, you should be provoked to hold conversations with colleagues about the dominant values and beliefs in your school and further obligated to challenge these principles as to how well they support children in your school. Moreover, upon discovery of any value or belief that is of poor service to the mission of educating every child, you are motivated to adopt principles that change your actions to advance the children's academic achievement.

Gademer (1991) posits that history does not belong to us; we belong to it. Within history, we find tradition—the act of handing down cultural traits such as values, beliefs, and practices from one generation to the next. The power of tradition is that it sanctions cultural acts and presents them to the next generation as unquestionable truths. The culturally proficient journey requires that educators question tradition, or, more forcefully stated, question the truth about how we educate children. We face a reality that many of us are educated by schools that created, maintained, and propagated

- racial segregation,
- gender inequality,
- academic tracking systems,
- religious disparities,
- homophobia, and/or
- ableism.

Facing this truth affords us the opportunity to interrupt tradition and purposefully stop the proliferation of indifference and create a culture of responsiveness and responsibility to one another. Our intent in this book is to prepare educators to unshackle themselves from tradition and become facilitators for reconciliation of historical injustices.

Dr. Martin Luther King, Jr. (1963) reminds us, "Never forget that everything Hitler did in Germany was legal." King's observation urges us to give attention to our moral obligation to humanity more so than legal mandates for forced responsibility. He helps us recognize that what we think and feel matters, and all in the law is not of the highest moral authority.

During his campaign for President of the United States of America, Senator Barack Obama's speech in Philadelphia echoes King's sentiment. He highlighted the importance of our responsibility for moral action in order to fully realize the promise of the ideals embedded in United States Constitution. Freedom and justice are moral principles that underpin this country's genesis. However, without our willingness to act from these principles, they are simply seeds without soil.

Words on a parchment would not be enough to deliver slaves from bondage, or provide men and women of every color and creed their full rights and obligations as citizens of the United States. What would be needed were Americans in successive generations who were willing to do their part—through protests and struggle, on the streets and in the courts, through a civil war and civil disobedience and always at great risk—to narrow the gap between the promise of our ideals and reality of their time. (Obama, 2009)

We encourage you to adopt the Principles of Cultural Proficiency, continue to practice self-reflection, and align your actions accordingly. In so doing, our expectation is that your journey will capture the opportunity that lies within King's (1998) statement, "Humankind has advanced technologically to conquer outer space, but humankind has not had the moral commitment to conquer their inner space".

—Franklin
—Brenda
—Randy

References

Adelman, Larry. (Producer). (2003). *Race: the power of an illusion* [Motion picture]. California Newsreel.

Argyris, Chris. (1990). *Overcoming organizational defenses: Facilitating organizational learning*. Needham, MA: Allyn & Bacon.

Barker, Joel. (Producer) (2001). *The new business of paradigms* [Motion picture]. Saint Paul, MN: Star Thrower Distribution.

Bennett, Lerone, Jr. (1987). *Before the mayflower: A history of black America*. Chicago: Johnson Publishing

Bohm, David. (1996). *On dialogue*. New York: Routledge.

Brookfield, Stephen. (2005). Learning democratic reason: The adult education project of Jurgen Habermas. *Teachers College Record, 107(6)*, 1127–1168.

Brown, Dee. (1972). *Bury my heart at Wounded Knee: An Indian history of the American West*. New York: Bantam Books.

CampbellJones, Brenda. (2002). *Against the stream: White men who act in ways to eradicate racism and white privilege/entitlement in the United States of America*. Unpublished doctoral dissertation, Claremont Graduate University, Los Angeles.

CampbellJones, Brenda, & CampbellJones, Franklin. (2002, Spring). Educating African-American children: Credibility at a crossroads. *Educational Horizons, 80(3)*, 133–139.

Cross, Terry L. (1989). *Toward a culturally competent system of care*. Washington DC: Georgetown University Child Development Program, Child and Adolescent Service System Program.

Delpit, Lisa. (1995). *Other people's children: Cultural conflict in the classroom*. New York: New Press.

Dyson, Michael Eric. (2008, April 6). *Meet the press*. [Television Program].

Ellinor, Linda, & Gerard, Glenna. (1998). *Dialogue: Rediscovering the transforming power of conversation*. New York: John Wiley.

Freire, Paulo. (1987). *Pedagogy of the heart*. New York: Continuum.

Fullan, Michael. (2003). *The moral imperative of school leadership*. Thousand Oaks, CA: Corwin.

Gadamer, Hans-Georg. (1991). *Truth and method* (2nd ed.). (J. Weinhsheimer & Marshall, D., Trans.). New York: Crossroad.

Gilligan, Carol. (1983). *In a different voice*. Cambridge, MA: Harvard University Press.

Gill-Monroe, Alicia. (2006). *Co-creation: Shifting the source of policy making*. Unpublished doctoral dissertation, Rowan University, Glassboro, New Jersey.

Gladwell, Malcolm. (2005). *Blink: The power of thinking without thinking*. New York: Little Brown

Habermas, Jurgen. (1990). *Moral consciousness and communicative action*. (Christian Lenhardt & Sherry Weber Nicholsen, Trans.). Cambridge, MA: MIT Press. (Original work published 1983)

Hehir, Thomas. (2002). Eliminating ableism in education. *Harvard Educational Review. 72(1)*, 1–32.

Hilliard, Asa. (1991). Do we have the will to educate all children? *Educational Leadership, 40*(1), 31–36.

Kempis, Thomas. (1980). *The imitation of Christ*. Chicago: Moody Press.

King, Martin Luther, Jr. (Speaker). (1998). *A knock at midnight: Inspiration from the great sermons of Reverend Martin Luther King, Jr.* (Cassette recording). New York: Time Warner Audio Books.

King, Martin Luther Jr. (1963, April 16). *Letter from a Birmingham Jail*. Atlanta, GA: The King Center. Retrieved June 10, 2009, from http://coursesa.matrix.msu.edu/~hst306/documents/letter.html

Kohlberg, Lawrence. (1973). The claim to moral adequacy of a highest stage of moral judgment. *The Journal of Philosophy, 70*(18), 630–646.

Kozol, Jonathan. (1991). *Savage inequalities: Children in America's schools*. New York: Crown.

Lindsey, Randall B., Nuri-Robins, Kikanza, & Terrell, Raymond. (2003). *Cultural Proficiency: A manual for school leaders* (2nd ed.). Thousand Oaks, CA: Corwin.

Lindsey, Randall B., Roberts, Laraine M., & CampbellJones, Franklin. (2005). *The culturally proficient school: An implementation guide for school leaders*. Thousand Oaks, CA: Corwin.

Low, W. Augustus, & Clift, Virgil A. (Eds.). (1981). *Encyclopedia of black America*. New York: McGraw-Hill.

Maturana, Humberto, & Varela, Francisco. (1992). *The tree of knowledge: The biological roots of human understanding*. Boston: Shambhala.

National Association of Educational Progress. *The nation's report card*. Available from http://nces.ed.gov/nationsreportcard/pubs/main2007/2007494.asp

NCLB. (2001). *No Child Left Behind Act*. Retrieved October 22, 2005, from http://www.ed.gov/nclb

Noli, Pam, & Jones, Franklin. (1996). *Creating a diversity-sensitive environment for powerful student learning*. California State Department of Education: Professional Learning Module for the California School Leadership Academy.

Nuri-Robins, Kikanza, Lindsey, Randall B., Lindsey, Delores B., & Terrell, Raymond D. (2006). *Culturally proficient instruction: A guide for people who teach* (2nd ed.) Thousand Oaks, CA: Corwin Press.

Perie, Marianne, Moran, Rebecca, & Lutkus, Anthony D. (2005). *NAEP 2004 trends in academic progress: Three decades of student performance in reading and mathematics (NCES 2005–464)*. U.S. Department of Education, Institute of Education Sciences, National Center for Education Statistics. Washington, DC: Government Printing Office.

Schein, Edgar H. (2004). *Organizational culture and leadership* (3rd ed.). San Francisco: Jossey-Bass.

Senge, Peter, Kleiner, Art, Roberts, Charlotte, Ross, Richard B., & Smith, Bryan S. (1994). *The fifth discipline field book: Strategies and tools for building a learning organization*. New York: Doubleday.

Senge, Peter, Kleiner, Art, Roberts, Charlotte, Roth, George, Ross, Richard B., & Smith, Bryan S. (1999). *The dance of change*. New York: Doubleday.

Sergiovanni, Thomas J. (1992). *Moral leadership: Getting to the heart of school improvement.* New York: Jossey-Bass.

Spring, Joel. (2000). *American education* (9th ed.). New York: McGraw-Hill.

Terrell, Raymond, & Lindsey, Randall B. (2009). *Culturally proficient leadership: The journey begins within.* Thousand Oaks, CA: Corwin.

The Educational Trust. (2006, September 12). Yes we can: Telling truths and dispelling myths about race and education in America. *The Education Trust.* Retrieved August 24, 2009, from http://www2.edtrust.org/EdTrust/Press+Room/Yes+We+Can.htm

Williamson, Marianne. (1992). *Return to love: Reflections on the principles of a course in Miracles.* New York: HarperCollins.

Woodson, Carter. (1933). *The miseducation of the negro.* Washington, DC: Associated Publishers.

Zohar, Danah. (1990). *The quantum self: Human nature and consciousness defined by the new physics.* New York: William Morrow.

Further Readings

Argyris, Chris. (1993). *Knowledge for action: A guide to overcoming barriers to organizational change.* San Francisco: Jossey-Bass.

Argyis, Chris, & Schon, Donald A. (1974). *Theory in practice.* San Francisco: Jossey-Bass.

Argyis, Chris, & Schon, Donald A. (1996). *Organizational learning* (Vol. 2). San Francisco: Jossey-Bass.

Banks, James. (1999). *An introduction to multicultural education* (3rd ed.). Needham, MA: Addison-Wesley.

Block, Peter. (2001). *The answer to how is yes.* San Francisco: Berrett-Koehler.

Bohn, Anita Petra, & Sleeter, Christine E. (2000). Multicultural education and the standards movement: A report from the field. *Kappan, 82*(2), 156–159.

Brown, John Seely, & Duguid, Paul. (2000). *The social life of information.* Cambridge, MA: Harvard Business School Press.

Brown, Juanita S., & Isaacs, David. (2001, June/July). The world café: living knowledge through conversations that matter: *The Systems Thinker,* 1–5.

Costa, Art L., & Garmston, Robert J. (2002). *Cognitive coaching: A foundation for renaissance schools* (2nd ed.). Norwood, MA: Christopher-Gordon.

Covey, Steven R. (1989). *The seven habits of highly effective people.* New York: Fireside.

Cross, Terry L., Bazaron, Barbara J., Dennis, Karl W., & Isaacs, Mareasa R. (1993). *Toward a culturally competent system of care* (Vol. 2). Washington, DC: Georgetown University Child Development Program. Child and Adolescent Service System Program.

DuFour, Richard, & Eaker, Robert. (1998). *Professional learning communities at work: Best practices for enhancing student achievement.* Alexandria, VA: Association for Supervision and Curriculum Development.

Dyer, Wayne, W. (2009) *Excuses be gone!: How to change lifelong self-defeating thinking and habits.* New York: Hay House.

Elmore, Richard. (2000). *Building a new structure for school leadership.* Washington, DC: Albert Shanker Institute.

Fashola, Olatokunbo S. (Ed.). (2005). *Educating African American males: Voices from the field.* Thousand Oaks, CA: Corwin.

Freire, Paulo. (1990). *Education for critical consciousness.* New York: Continuum.

Freire, Paulo. (1999). *Pedagogy of hope: Reliving pedagogy of the oppressed.* New York: Continuum.

Fullan, Michael. (1991). *The new meaning of educational change*. New York: Teachers College Press.

Garcia, Eugene. (1999). *Student cultural diversity: Understanding and meeting the challenge*. Boston: Houghton Mifflin.

Gladwell, Malcolm. (2000). *The tipping point: How little things can make a big difference*. Boston: Little, Brown.

Goleman, Daniel. (1995). *Emotional intelligence*. New York: Bantam.

Gollnick, Donna M., & Chinn, Phillip C. (1990). *Multicultural education in a pluralistic society*. Englewood Cliffs, NJ: Prentice Hall.

Gordon, Milton M. (1964). *Assimilation in American life: The role of race, religion, and national origins*. New York: Oxford University Press.

Graham, Stephanie, & Lindsey, Randall B. (2002, March/April). Balance and power: *Leadership*, 20–23.

Habermas, Jurgen. (1975). *Legitimation crisis*. Boston, MA: Beacon Press.

Heifetz, Ronald A. (1994). *Leadership without easy answers*. Cambridge, MA: Belknap.

Herda, Ellen A. (1999). *Research conversations and narrative: A critical hermeneutic orientation in participatory inquiry*. Westport, CT: Praeger.

Jones, Franklin Lawrence. (1993). *Project pipeline: A hermeneutic approach for recruiting underrepresented American mathematics and science teachers into the public school workforce*. Unpublished doctoral dissertation, University of San Francisco.

Kohlberg, Lawrence, & Hersh, Richard H. (1977). Moral development: A review of the theory. *Theory into Practice, 16*(2), 53–59.

Kovel, Joel. (1984). *White racism: A psychohistory*. New York: Columbia University Press.

Ladson-Billings, Gloria. (1994). *The dreamkeepers: Successful teachers of African-American children*. San Francisco: Jossey-Bass.

Lindsey, Delores B., Martinez, Richard S., & Lindsey, Randall B. (2007). *Culturally proficient coaching: Supporting educators to create equitable schools*. Thousand Oaks, CA: Corwin.

Maeroff, Gene. (1999). *Altered destinies: Making life better for school children in need*. New York: St. Martin's.

Myrdal, Gunnar. (1994). *An American dilemma: The Negro problem and modern democracy*. New York: Pantheon.

Nieto, Sonia. (2000). Affirming diversity: *The sociopolitical context of multicultural education* (3rd ed.). Reading, MA: Addison-Wesley.

Ogbu, John. (1992). Understanding cultural diversity and learning. *Educational Researcher, 21*(8), 5–14.

Reeves, Douglas B. (2000). *Accountability in action: A blueprint for learning organizations*. Denver, CO: Center for Performance Assessment.

Senge, Peter, Cambron, Nelda H., McCabe, Timothy Lucas, Kleiner, Art, Dutton, Janis, & Smith, Bryan. (2000). *Schools that learn: A fifth discipline field book for educators, parents, and everyone who cares about education*. New York: Doubleday.

Sergiovanni, Thomas J. (2001). *The principalship: A reflective practice perspective* (4th ed.). Boston: Allyn & Bacon.

Shapiro, Joan Poliner, & Stefkovich, Jacqueline A. (2005). *Ethical leadership and decision making in education: Applying theoretical perspectives to complex dilemmas*. Mahwah, NJ: Lawrence Erlbaum Associates.

Sheets, Rosa Hernandez. (2000). Advancing the field or taking center stage: The white movement in multicultural education. *Educational Researcher, 29*(9), 15–20.

Spring, Joel. (2004). *American school 1642–2004* (6th ed.). Boston: McGraw-Hill.

Takaki, Ronald. (1993). *A different mirror: A history of multicultural America.* Boston: Little Brown.

Takaki, Ronald. (1998). *A larger memory: A history of our diversity with voices.* Boston: Little Brown

Tatum, Beverly Daniel. (1999). Why are all the black kids sitting together in the cafeteria? New York: Basic Books.

Terry, Robert. (1970). *For whites only.* Grand Rapids, MI: Eerdmans.

Wheatley, Margaret J. (2002). *Turning to one another: Simple conversations to restore hope to the future.* San Francisco: Berrett-Koehler.

Zander, Benjamin, & Zander, Rosamund Stone. (2000). *The art of possibility: Transforming professional and personal life.* Cambridge, MA: Harvard Business School Press.

Zohar, Danah & Marshall, Ian. (2004). *Spiritual capital: Wealth we can live by.* San Francisco: Berrett-Koehler

Index

CORWIN

A SAGE Company

The Corwin logo—a raven striding across an open book—represents the union of courage and learning. Corwin is committed to improving education for all learners by publishing books and other professional development resources for those serving the field of PreK–12 education. By providing practical, hands-on materials, Corwin continues to carry out the promise of its motto: **"Helping Educators Do Their Work Better."**